S0-FPI-995

ABACUS
BRANDS

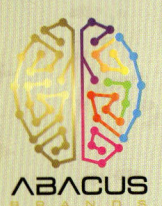

This edition published in 2023 by
Abacus Brands, Inc.
5501 Balcones Dr, Suite-A211,
Austin, TX 78731
USA

CEO & Creative Direction: Steve Rad
Project Manager: Sydnie Hyde, Angela Chen, Jordyn Van de Keere
Art Direction: Ingrid Chow
Design & Illustration: Ingrid Chow, Linda Tran, Fraser Aberdeen, Dionysis Zogaris, Hanna Stefan, Alla Gindullina
Photo & Video: Rami Mikhail
Packaging Photography: Vishal Klair
Editorial: Eleanor Rose, Alan Bo, Aaron Carr
Copy Editor: Sue Vander Hook
Sourcing & Production: Jack Xing, Philip Tien
App Design & Interface: Jeff Dotson, Tony Fouts, Brian Massey, Christopher Brown, Jacob Jetter, Jeremy Schaefer, Ryan Hanson, Austin Hancock, Angie Antoine
Content & Licensing: Levin Nelson
Animation: Daniel Mandina
3D Artist: Devon Carlson

UPC: 850009794345
ISBN: 978-1-951090-11-1

Manufactured in China

Patent # 10430658, 10558858, 10565452

Edition: 03.ABA94345.0323
Copyright © Abacus Brands™ 2023
Virtual Reality World Atlas™ is the registered trademark of Abacus Brands, Inc.
All rights reserved.

No part of this book may be reproduced, stored in a retrieval system or transmitted in any form or by any means, electronic, mechanical, photocopying, recording, or otherwise, without the prior written permission of the publishers and copyright holders.

Special thanks to:
Jackie McCoy-Rad, Alexander Maxwell Rad, Ayla Jordan Rad, Ken Vannucci, Sara Carinchi, Kira Freed, Kristin Templin

VIRTUAL REALITY
WORLD ATLAS!

Point the app at the Abacus Brands logo to unlock a secret VR experience!

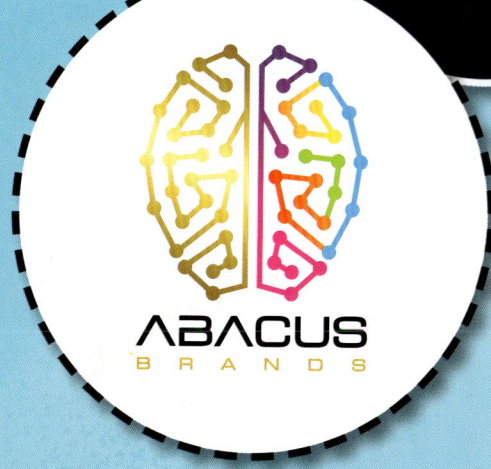

ABACUS BRANDS

@ABACUSBRANDS
ABACUSBRANDS.COM

CONTENTS

6 Getting Started

7 General Safety

8 Our World

10 North America
- 12 USA
- 14 Canada
- 16 Mexico
- 18 Central America
- 19 Caribbean
- 20 Wonders of the World
- 21 Earth's Climates

22 South America
- 24 Colombia & Venezuela
- 25 Ecuador & Peru
- 26 Brazil
- 28 Argentina & Chile

30 Europe
- 32 Portugal & Spain
- 34 British Isles
- 36 France
- 38 The Netherlands & Belgium
- 39 Switzerland & Austria
- 40 Germany
- 42 Italy
- 44 The Nordics
- 46 Poland, Czech Republic, Slovakia
- 48 Hungary & Croatia
- 49 Ukraine
- 50 Romania & Bulgaria
- 51 Greece
- 52 Russia (Europe)
- 54 Most Visted Cities
- 55 Tallest Buildings & Longest Bridges

56 Africa
- 58 Morocco & Algeria
- 59 Tunisia & Libya
- 60 Egypt
- 61 Ethiopia & Kenya
- 62 Ivory Coast & Ghana
- 63 Nigeria
- 64 Congo (DRC)
- 65 Zambia & Zimbabwe
- 66 South Africa
- 67 Madagascar

Santorini
Greece

Grand Canyon
Arizona, USA

Moai
Easter Island, Chile

68 Asia

- 70 Turkey
- 72 Kazakhstan & Russia (Asia)
- 74 Israel & Jordan
- 75 Syria & Lebanon
- 76 Persian Gulf
- 78 Iran
- 79 Afghanistan & Pakistan
- 80 India & Sri Lanka
- 82 Nepal & Bangladesh
- 83 Myanmar
- 84 Southeast Asia
- 86 Southeast Asia continued
- 88 China & Mongolia
- 90 North Korea & South Korea
- 92 Japan
- 94 From High to Low
- 95 Wonderful Water

96 Oceania

- 98 Australia
- 100 New Zealand

102 The Polar Regions

- 102 Antarctica
- 104 The Arctic

106 World Highlights

108 More to Explore

Each country contains unique VR content from around the world! Look at any country map to activate the experience!

Great Barrier Reef
Queensland, Australia

Arctic Ice
The Arctic

Scratch off countries on the scratch map as you globetrot in virtual reality!

GETTING STARTED

1 Download the **VIRTUAL REALITY WORLD ATLAS** app in either the Apple or Google Play store.

2 Hit **START**, and place your device into the included goggles. Simply point and look at any country map to activate the VR experience.

3 While in virtual reality, use the reticle (blue dot in the center) to point and play options inside the virtual room.

4 To exit virtual reality, point at the **BACK** button found below near your feet. Then, flip to any country map to activate a new experience.

TIPS & TRICKS

- Give the app permission to use your camera.
- Be sure your ringer switch is on and not set to silent.
- Turn up the brightness of your screen.
- Disable auto-brightness to prevent dimming during the experience.
- Wipe smudges and fingerprints from your device.
- Use standard or mid-size phones as larger devices may not fit properly.
- Remove your phone's protective case when possible.

Be sure to adjust the eye controls at the bottom to align focus.

FREQUENTLY ASKED QUESTIONS

Which devices are compatible?
We recommend a mobile device for Android version 7.0 or greater or Apple iPhone 6S or better, running iOS version 9.0 or greater. Tablets can be used for AR full screen lessons only, as they do not trigger VR experiences and cannot fit inside the goggles.

How do I exit virtual reality?
When in VR, a floating "exit" button can be found near your feet. Use the blue dot in the center of the screen to point and activate the exit feature.

Visit us online at abacusbrands.com/pages/faqs for more frequently asked questions, or email us directly at support@abacusbrands.com to troubleshoot any issues you may be experiencing. We are happy to help!

GENERAL SAFETY

- Avoid watching all the VR content consecutively as extended use can lead to eye strain.
- We recommend periodic breaks, as looking at digital devices for over 15 minutes can make your eyes sore, itchy, tired, or watery.
- Stop using virtual reality if you experience discomfort, disorientation, or nausea.
- Avoid walking or moving while using virtual reality.
- Do not leave the virtual reality viewer in direct sunlight.

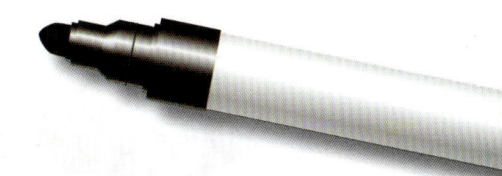

OUR WORLD

7 continents, 195 countries and regions, over 4,400 cities — our world is a big and wondrous place. This interactive atlas highlights incredible sights, sounds, and flavors from around the planet.

NORTH AMERICA
Countries | 23
Largest Country | Canada
Largest Population | USA

Equator

SOUTH AMERICA
Countries | 12
Largest Country | Brazil
Largest Population | Brazil

Your Digital Experience Starts Now!

Hit **START** in the app, and point at pages **8 AND 9**.

ANTARCTICA
Countries | 0
Largest Country | NA
Largest Population | NA

8 OUR WORLD

EUROPE
Countries | 44
Largest Country | Russia
Largest Population | Russia

ASIA
Countries | 48
Largest Country | Russia
Largest Population | China

OCEANIA
Countries | 14
Largest Country | Australia
Largest Population | Australia

AFRICA
Countries | 54
Largest Country | Algeria
Largest Population | Nigeria

OUR WORLD

NORTH AMERICA

Metropolitan cities amid vast wilderness and stunning islands across the Caribbean Sea

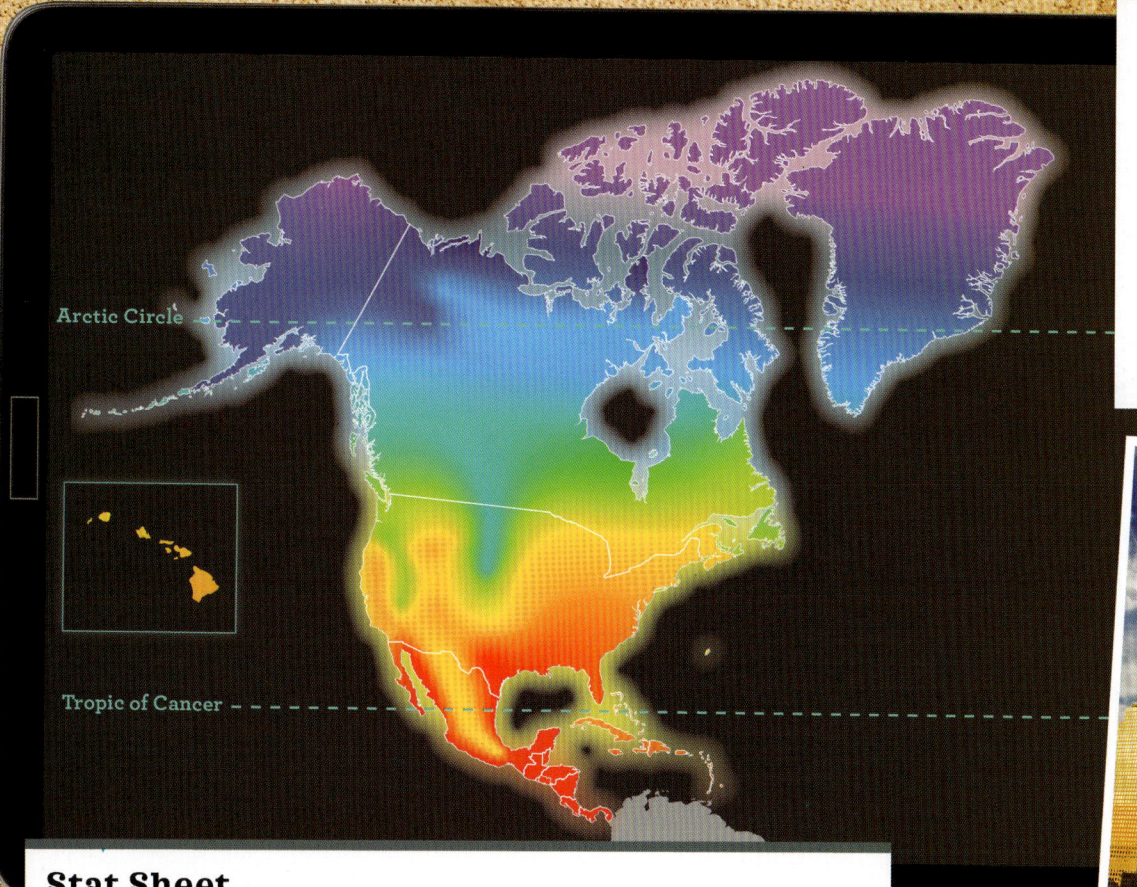

Average Temperatures

- 86°F+ (30°C+)
- 77°F (25°C)
- 68°F (20°C)
- 59°F (15°C)
- 50°F (10°C)
- 41°F (5°C)
- 32°F (0°C)
- 14°F (-10°C)
- -4°F (-20°C)

One World Trade Center – New York City, USA

Stat Sheet
Total Area | 9.54M mi² (24.71M km²)
Largest Crop Export | Corn
Highest Mountain | Denali (USA) 20,310 ft (6,190 m)
Longest River | Mississippi-Missouri River (USA) 3,710 mi (5,970 km)
Largest Lake | Lake Superior 31,700 mi² (82,103 km²)
Longest Coastline | Canada 151,019 mi (202,080 km)
Tallest Building | One World Trade Center (USA) 1,780 ft (541 m)

Lake Superior – Canada and USA

Denali – Alaska, USA

Population Density

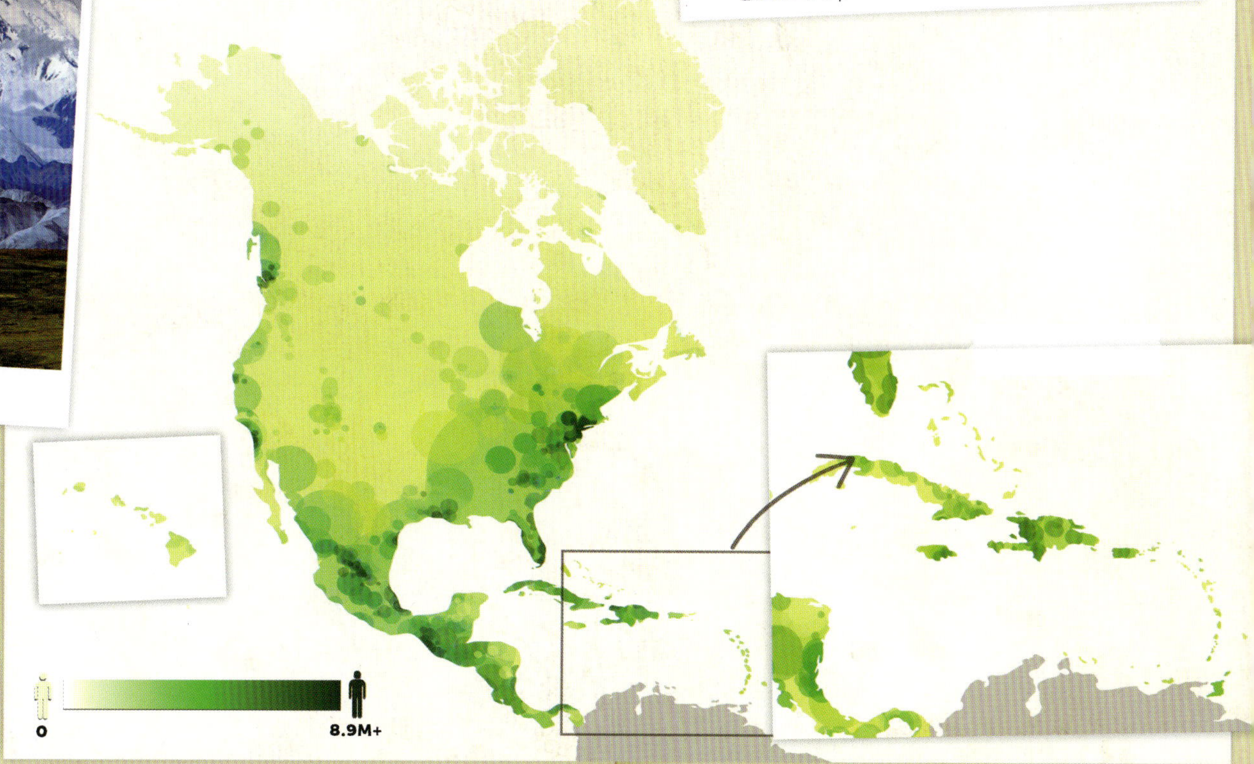

0 — 8.9M+

NORTH AMERICA
11

USA

High mountains and low swamps, big burgers and grand canyons, space needles and space flights are just a few highlights of this diverse country.

Capital | Washington, DC
Population | Approx. 329M
Language | English

Space Needle
Seattle's iconic observation tower opened in 1962.

Mount St. Helens
An active volcano in the Cascade mountain range

Yellowstone National Park
The oldest national park in the USA and home to the famous geyser Old Faithful

Seattle
Olympia
WASHINGTON
Portland
Salem
OREGON
Helena
MONTANA
Boise
IDAHO
ROCKY MOUNTAINS
WYOMING

Mount Rushmore
The heads of four American presidents are carved into this mountain.

ALASKA
Juneau

Purchased from the Russian Empire at a cost of 2 cents per acre, Alaska became the 49th state in 1959.

Golden Gate Bridge
San Francisco is home to the most photographed bridge in the world.

Sacramento
Carson City
San Francisco
NEVADA
GREAT BASIN DESERT
Salt Lake City
UTAH
Cheyenne
Denver
COLORADO

Yosemite Falls
The tallest waterfall in North America

Arches National Park
Over 2,000 natural stone arches form a striking red landscape.

CALIFORNIA
Las Vegas
MOJAVE DESERT
Grand Canyon
Santa Fe
Route 66

Great White Shark
Great whites live in the Pacific Ocean, from Mexico up to the Gulf of Alaska.

Los Angeles
HOLLYWOOD
San Diego
ARIZONA
Phoenix
SONORAN DESERT
Tucson
Albuquerque
NEW MEXICO
El Paso

Route 66
This historic highway passes through eight states, stretching from Illinois to California.

Hollywood Sign
Landmark in Los Angeles, a city famous for creating movies and TV shows

HAWAII
Honolulu
Aloha

The 50th state, made up of eight major islands (and 137 total islands), is a tropical paradise.

Cheeseburger and Fries

Grand Canyon
Formed by the Colorado River over millions of years

Hey

Cuisine
Well-known American dishes include burgers, shakes, fries, and fried chicken.

One-Dollar Bill

12 NORTH AMERICA – USA

Liberty Bell
Bells rang in Philadelphia to celebrate America's independence in 1776.

American Sports
Popular sports include American football, basketball, and baseball.

Basketball
Golf
Baseball
American Football

Willis Tower
This tower has the highest observation deck in the country.

Statue of Liberty
A gift from France, the statue depicts Libertas, the Roman goddess of liberty!

Empire State Building
The world's tallest building from 1931 to 1970

Lake of the Ozarks
A huge reservoir in Missouri with more shoreline than the coast of California

Elvis Presley
Known as the King of Rock and Roll

Martin Luther King Jr.
A minister and activist who led the Civil Rights Movement

Kennedy Space Center
NASA launches its human spaceflight missions from this site.

Mardi Gras
Annual carnival in New Orleans celebrating shrove or "Fat Tuesday"

Walt Disney World® Resort
"The most magical place on Earth" opened in 1971.

States and Cities
- NORTH DAKOTA — Bismarck
- MINNESOTA — Minneapolis, St. Paul
- WISCONSIN — Madison
- MICHIGAN — Lansing, Detroit
- MAINE — Augusta
- VERMONT
- NEW HAMPSHIRE
- MASSACHUSETTS — Boston
- NEW YORK — Albany, New York City
- RHODE ISLAND
- CONNECTICUT
- SOUTH DAKOTA — Pierre
- IOWA — Des Moines
- ILLINOIS — Chicago, Springfield
- INDIANA — Indianapolis
- OHIO — Columbus, Cleveland
- PENNSYLVANIA — Harrisburg, Philadelphia
- NEW JERSEY
- DELAWARE
- MARYLAND
- NEBRASKA — Lincoln
- MISSOURI — Jefferson City
- KENTUCKY — Frankfort
- WEST VIRGINIA
- VIRGINIA — Richmond
- The White House — Washington, DC
- KANSAS — Topeka
- OKLAHOMA — Oklahoma City
- ARKANSAS — Little Rock
- TENNESSEE — Nashville
- NORTH CAROLINA — Raleigh, Charlotte
- SOUTH CAROLINA — Columbia, Charleston
- GEORGIA — Atlanta
- TEXAS — Dallas, Austin, Houston, San Antonio
- LOUISIANA — Baton Rouge, New Orleans
- MISSISSIPPI — Jackson
- ALABAMA — Montgomery
- FLORIDA — Tallahassee, Orlando, Miami

APPALACHIAN MOUNTAINS
Atlantic Ocean
Gulf of Mexico
Teepee
Shawl Dancer

New York City
America's epicenter of fashion, finance, dining, and shopping

Native Americans
The indigenous peoples of the USA are known as Native Americans. More than 500 distinct tribes live throughout the country. Groups include the Sioux, Cherokee, Apache, and Navajo.

Holidays
Holidays include Easter, Independence Day, Halloween, and Thanksgiving

NORTH AMERICA – USA

CANADA

This wonderland spans a vast distance. Far and wide, Canadians share a love of winter sports and natural beauty.

Capital | Ottawa
Population | Approx. 37M
Languages | English, French

Grizzly Bears
Before hibernation, grizzlies can gain up to 400 lbs eating everything from bees to salmon.

Gold
Gold was discovered in the Yukon in 1896.

Totem Poles
Carvings created by First Nations to represent history, people, and events

Dinosaur Provincial Park
World's richest dinosaur fossil site

Calgary Stampede
A world-famous rodeo event that takes place in July

Ice Hockey
Ice hockey is the nation's official winter sport. Both the men's and women's teams have won more Olympic gold medals in ice hockey than any other country.

Rocky Mountains
The Rockies are home to snow-capped peaks and turquoise glacial lakes.

Cuisine
Well-known Canadian food includes poutine, smoked salmon, and Nanaimo bars.

Map labels: Arctic Ocean, Alaska (USA), Yukon, Whitehorse, Northwest Territories, Yellowknife, Nunavut, British Columbia, Rocky Mountains, Alberta, Saskatchewan, Saskatoon, Calgary, Regina, Vancouver, Victoria, Pacific Ocean

Moose: "Hello"

Other labels: Lacrosse, Curling, Hockey Player, Poutine

14 NORTH AMERICA – CANADA

Language and Nationality

Most people in America speak English. But American people come from many different countries. They speak different languages. They are different nationalities.

Read the words below the pictures. Answer the questions at the bottom of the page.

Tomas Hernandez is from Mexico.
He speaks Spanish. His nationality is Mexican.

Puri Mendiola is from the Philippines.
She speaks Tagalog. Her nationality is Filipino.

David Price is from Canada.
He speaks English. His nationality is Canadian.

Linda Minoso is from Cuba.
She speaks Spanish. Her nationality is Cuban.

Country, Language, and Nationality

Write the answers on the lines below.

1. Where is Tomas Hernandez from? __Mexico_____

2. What language does he speak? _____

3. Where is Linda Minoso from? _____

4. What is her nationality? _____

5. What language does David Price speak? _____

Learning a New Language / 23

Review Activity

Map Work: Countries, Languages, and Nationalities

Write the name of the country, language, and nationality on the lines below.

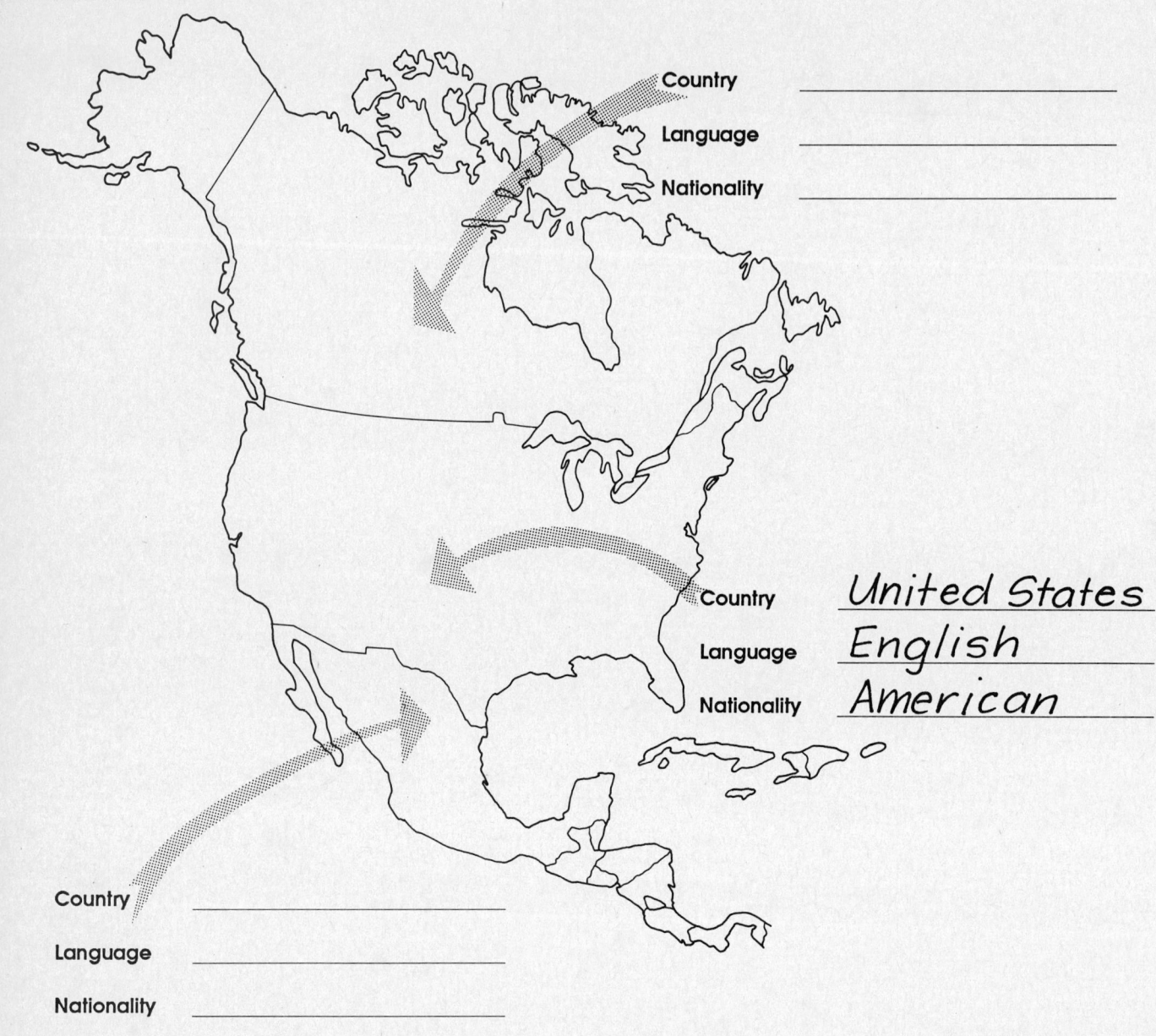

Country _____
Language _____
Nationality _____

Country <u>United States</u>
Language <u>English</u>
Nationality <u>American</u>

Country _____
Language _____
Nationality _____

Your Country, Language and Nationality

Write about yourself on the lines below.

1. What country do you come from? _____

2. Is your country on this map? _____

3. What language do you speak? _____

4. What nationality are you? _____

24 / *Here to Stay in the USA*

UNIT THREE

Time and the Seasons

Reading 1
Daily Activities

Key Words and Phrases

| wake up | cook | breakfast | go | work |
| get off | school | come home | A.M. | P.M. |

1 Teresa wakes up at 6:15 A.M.

2 She cooks breakfast at 6:45 A.M.

3 She goes to work at 7:30 A.M.

4 She gets off work at 4:30 P.M.

5 She goes to school at 6:30 P.M.

6 She comes home at 9:45 P.M.

26 / *Here to Stay in the USA*

Reading 2
Days of the Week

Key Words and Phrases

Monday	Tuesday	Wednesday	Thursday	Friday
Saturday	Sunday	work	night	study
bowling	visit	afternoon	home	family

1. Oscar works Monday to Friday.
2. On Tuesday night, he studies English.
3. He studies English on Thursday, too.
4. On Wednesday night, he goes bowling.
5. On Saturday night, he and Teresa visit friends.
6. On Sunday afternoon, he is home with his family.

Time and the Seasons / 27

Vocabulary Pictures
Time and the Seasons

Look at the pictures below. Circle the correct letter under each picture.

(a.) morning
b. afternoon
c. evening

a. morning
b. afternoon
c. evening

a. morning
b. afternoon
c. evening

a. winter
b. spring
c. summer
d. fall

a. winter
b. spring
c. summer
d. fall

a. winter
b. spring
c. summer
d. fall

a. winter
b. spring
c. summer
d. fall

Word Lists

Study these words with your classmates.

Days of the Week

Name	Abbreviations	
Sunday	Sun.	Su
Monday	Mon.	M
Tuesday	Tues.	T
Wednesday	Wed.	W
Thursday	Thurs.	Th
Friday	Fri.	F
Saturday	Sat.	S

Months of the Year

#	Name	Abbreviation	#	Name	Abbreviation
1	January	Jan.	7	July	Jul.
2	February	Feb.	8	August	Aug.
3	March	Mar.	9	September	Sept.
4	April	Apr.	10	October	Oct.
5	May	May	11	November	Nov.
6	June	Jun.	12	December	Dec.

yesterday ⤺ today ⤻ tomorrow

28 / *Here to Stay in the USA*

Action Scripts

The Day, the Time, the Year

Script 1 *Calendar*
(Materials: calendar and pencil)

1. Circle the first day of the month.

2. Write an **X** on the last Friday of the month.

3. Draw a line through all the Saturdays.

4. Circle the 15th of the month.

5. Write the name of the month.

			August			
S	M	T	W	T	F	S
			1	2	3	4
5	6	7	8	9	10	11
12	13	14	15	16	17	18
19	20	21	22	23	24	25
26	27	28	29	30	31	

Script 2 *Time*
(Materials: pencil)

Your teacher will tell you the time. Draw hands on the clocks to show the time.

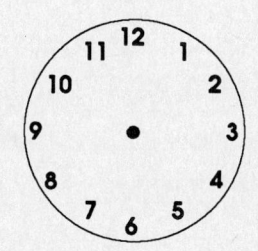

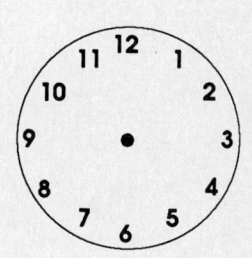

Script 3 *Years*
(Materials: chalkboard, chalk)

1. Write your date of birth on the chalkboard.

2. Write today's date on the chalkboard.

3. Write yesterday's date on the chalkboard.

4. Write tomorrow's date on the chalkboard.

5. Write the year you came to the U.S.A.

Time and the Seasons / 29

The Calendar

Look at the calendars. Answer the questions under the calendars.

February 1990						
S	M	T	W	T	F	S
				1	2	3
4	5	6	7	8	9	10
11	12	13	14	15	16	17
18	19	20	21	22	23	24
25	26	27	28			

March 1991						
S	M	T	W	T	F	S
					1	2
3	4	5	6	7	8	9
10	11	12	13	14	15	16
17	18	19	20	21	22	23
24	25	26	27	28	29	30
31						

April 1992						
S	M	T	W	T	F	S
			1	2	3	4
5	6	7	8	9	10	11
12	13	14	15	16	17	18
19	20	21	22	23	24	25
26	27	28	29	30		

Reading a Calendar

Write the answers on the lines below.

1. What day is March 3? ___Sunday___

2. What day is February 9? _____

3. What day is April 23? _____

4. What day is April 2? _____

5. February 9, 1990 is the same as ___2/9/90___

6. March 17, 1991 is the same as _____

7. 4/17/92 is the same as _____

8. 2/02/90 is the same as _____

What about You?

Write about yourself on the lines below.

1. What time do you wake up? _____

2. What time do you eat breakfast? _____

3. What time do you go to work? _____

4. What time do you eat dinner? _____

5. What time do you go to sleep? _____

Mr. __Oscar Gomez__

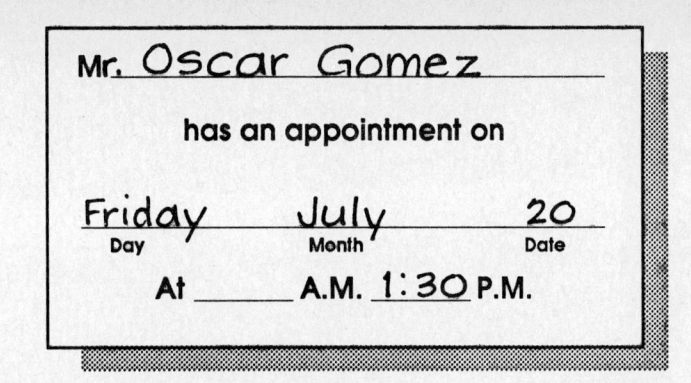

has an appointment on

__Friday__   __July__   __20__
Day   Month   Date

At _____ A.M. __1:30__ P.M.

Listen to This!

Your teacher will read the sentences below. Listen and circle the right answer in each box.

1. Your appointment is on Monday, [August 5 / October 5] at [10:00 / 11:00] A.M.

2. Your appointment is on Wednesday, [September 17 / December 17] at [12:30 / 3:30] P.M.

3. Your appointment is on Thursday, [July 16 / June 17] at [1:00 / 12:00] P.M.

4. Your appointment is on Saturday, [April 5 / May 5] at [4:45 P.M. / 6:45 A.M.]

5. Your appointment is on Friday, [February 18 / February 8] at [5:15 P.M. / 7:15 A.M.]

Conversation and Cooperation

Marissa's Daily Schedule

Work with a group of classmates. Write a daily schedule for Marissa.

6:30 A.M. _____

7:30 A.M. _____

9:30 A.M. _____

12:00 P.M. _____

5:45 P.M. _____

7:30 P.M. _____

11:30 P.M. _____

Time and the Seasons / 31

Time Talk

Read the dialogs below. Practice them with a classmate.

- It's 6:45.
- What time is it?
- Do you work tomorrow?
- No, I worked yesterday.
- What time is your class?
- From 7:00 to 9:00 tonight.
- Will you go to Mexico next month?
- No, I'll go next year.

32 / *Here to Stay in the USA*

What's in the Picture?

In the Kitchen

Talk about the picture with your classmates and teacher.

Student Space

Write your own words here.

Time and the Seasons / 33

Communication Strategies

> When you make an appointment, be sure to **clarify** the day, time, and date.

Can you come to the store next Wednesday?

Wednesday, December 20?

The plane arrives at 5:15 on the 4th.

5:15 P.M. on Thursday, the 4th?

The doctor will see you at the same time on Friday.

Friday, the 20th?

Be here at 3:30.

3:30 on April 25?

34 / *Here to Stay in the USA*

Holidays in America

An important American holiday is July Fourth. July Fourth is Independence Day. It is America's birthday.

Look at the pictures and calendars below. Circle the correct date for the American holiday on the calendar. Then write the date under the calendar.

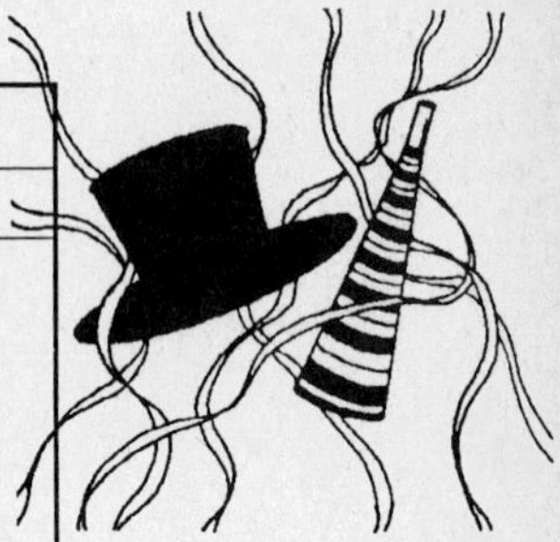

Independence Day   July 4th

New Year's Day _____

Martin Luther King Day _____

Memorial Day _____

Labor Day _____

Thanksgiving _____

Time and the Seasons / 35

American Time Zones

Look at the map. Do the exercises under the map.

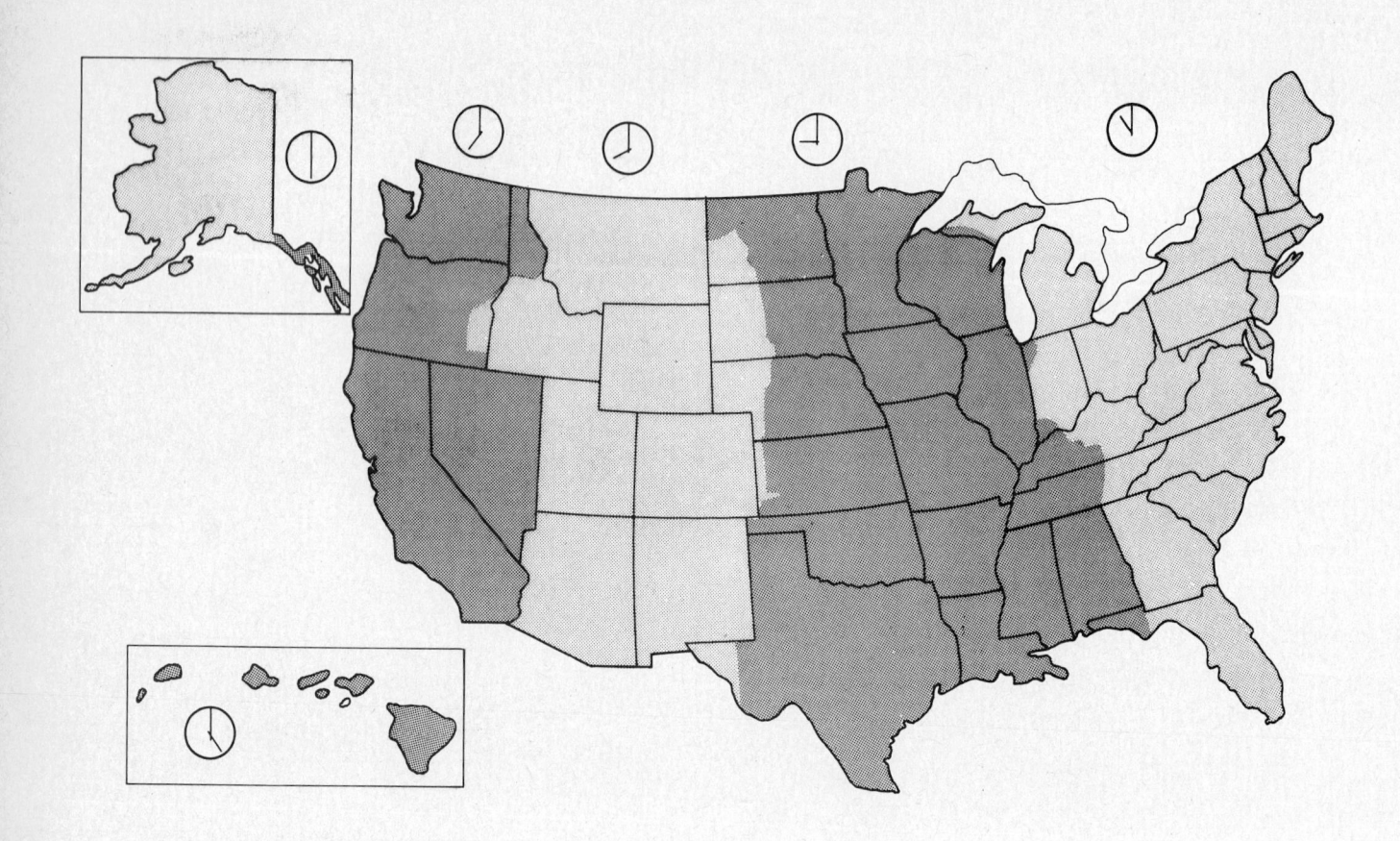

What Time Is It Here?

Write the correct times on the lines below.

9:00 A.M. in New York = _____ in California

3:00 P.M. in Chicago = _____ in California

11:00 A.M. in Los Angeles = _____ in New York

4:00 P.M. in Houston = _____ in Washington, D.C.

2:30 P.M. in Miami = _____ in Chicago

2:00 P.M. in Miami = _____ in Los Angeles

Review Activity

Answer the questions on the lines below.

yesterday ⟵ today ⟶ tomorrow

1. What day is today? _____

2. What day is tomorrow? _____

3. What day was yesterday? _____

4. What is today's date? _____

5. What is tomorrow's date? _____

36 / *Here to Stay in the USA*

UNIT FOUR

Your Community

Reading 1

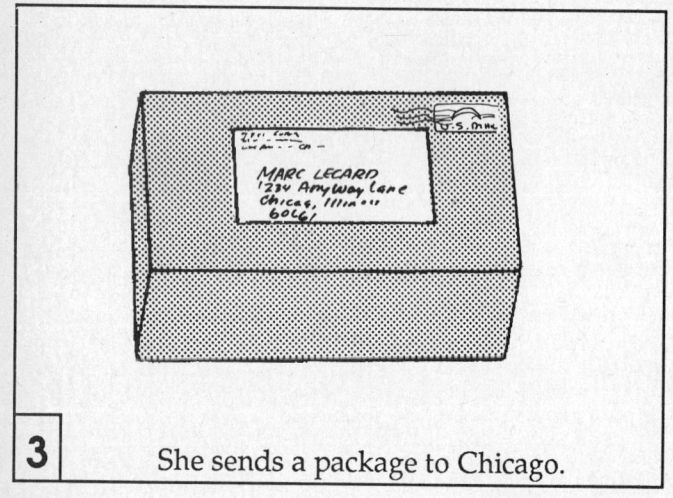

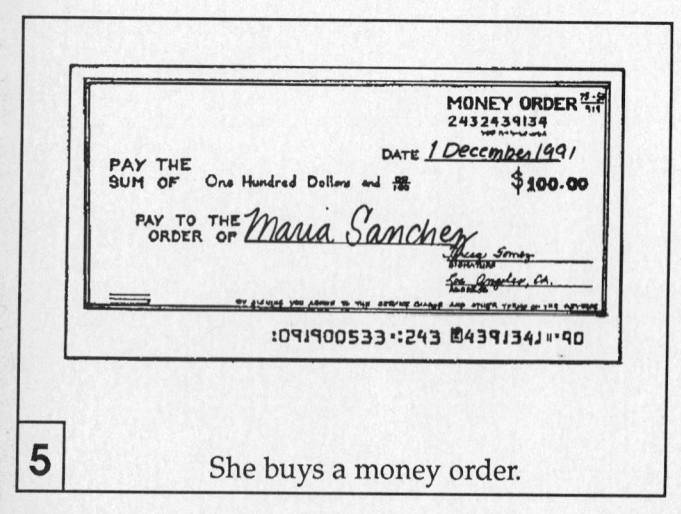

At the Post Office

Key Words and Phrases

| post office | mail | letter | send |
| package | buy | air mail stamps | money order |

1 Teresa is at the post office.

2 She mails a letter to Mexico.

3 She sends a package to Chicago.

4 She buys air mail stamps.

5 She buys a money order.

6 She sends the money order to Mexico.

38 / *Here to Stay in the USA*

Reading 2

An Accident

Key Words and Phrases

outside	see	accident	pay phone
call	911	say	name

1. Teresa is outside the post office.
2. She sees an accident. 
3. She goes to a pay phone. 
4. She calls 911. 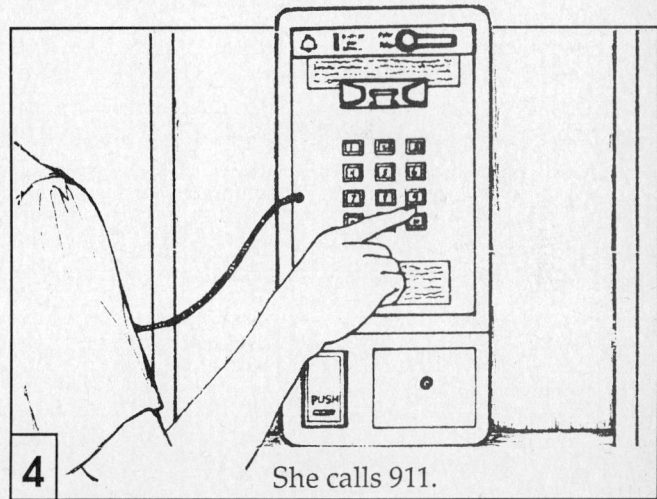
5. She says, "My name is Teresa Gomez." 
6. "There is a car accident at Wilshire Boulevard and Broadway."

Vocabulary Pictures
Community Services

Read the words below the pictures. Answer the questions at the bottom of the page.

Go to the **post office** to buy stamps.

Call the **police/911** to report an accident.

Go to the **library** to borrow a book.

Go to the **laundromat** to wash clothes.

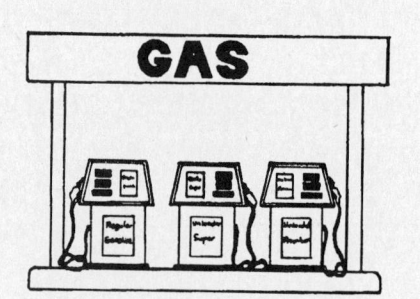

Go to the **gas station** to buy gas.

Go to the **bank** to cash a check.

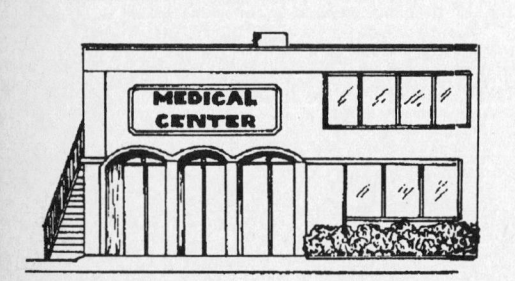

Go to the **medical clinic** to see a doctor.

Go to the **restaurant** to eat.

Go to the **supermarket** to buy food.

Where Do You Go?

Write the answer on the lines below.

1. Where do you wash your clothes? _laundromat_

2. Where do you buy stamps? _____

3. Where do you buy food? _____

4. Where do you buy gas? _____

5. Where do you see a doctor? _____

40 / *Here to Stay in the USA*

Action Scripts
The Phone Book

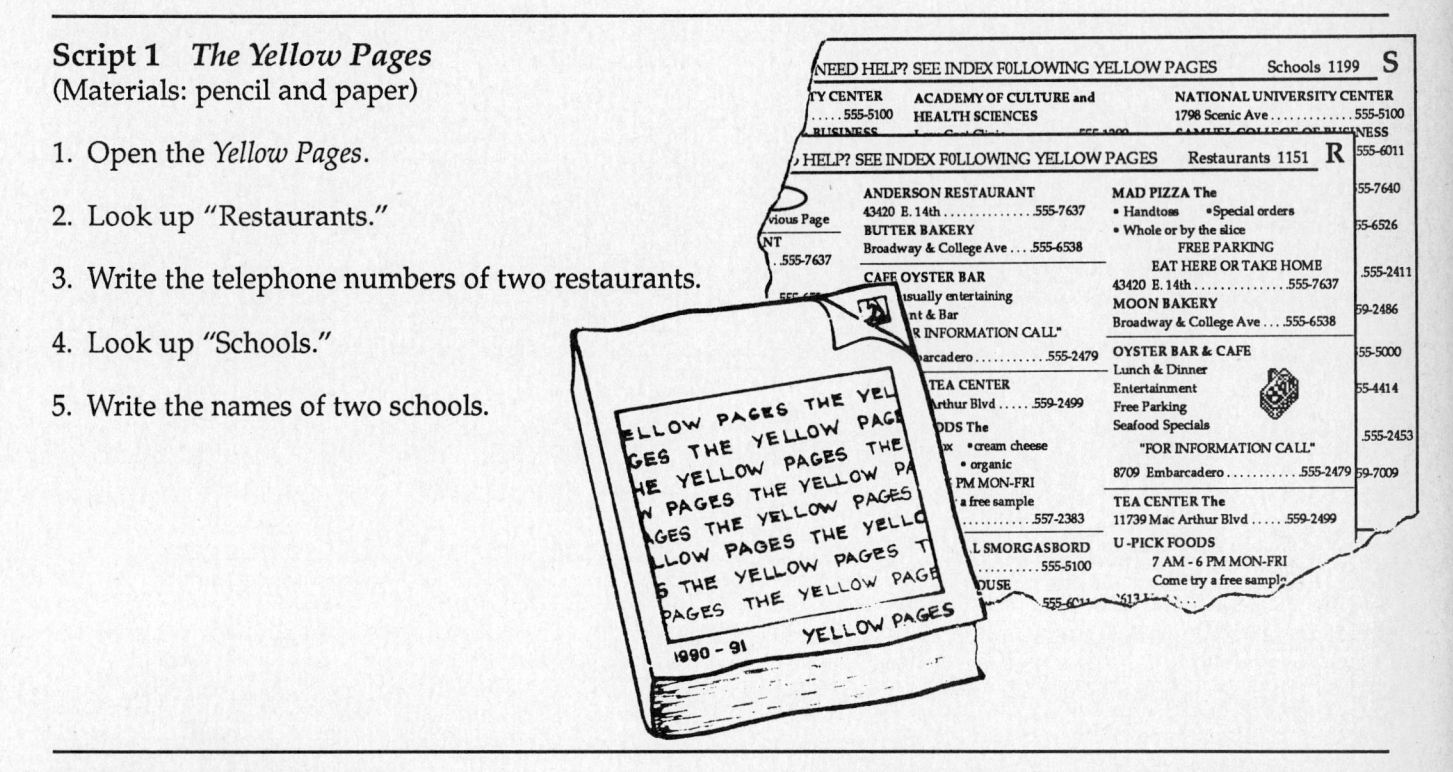

Script 1 *The Yellow Pages*
(Materials: pencil and paper)

1. Open the *Yellow Pages*.

2. Look up "Restaurants."

3. Write the telephone numbers of two restaurants.

4. Look up "Schools."

5. Write the names of two schools.

Script 2 *The White Pages*
(Materials: pencil and paper)

1. Open the *White Pages*.

2. Look up the letter "G."

3. Find a name beginning with "G." Write it down.

4. Write the person's telephone number.

5. Look up the letter "R."

6. Find a name beginning with "R." Write it down.

7. Write the person's address.

8. Write the person's telephone number.

Your Community / 41

Community Map

Look at the map. Answer the questions under the map.

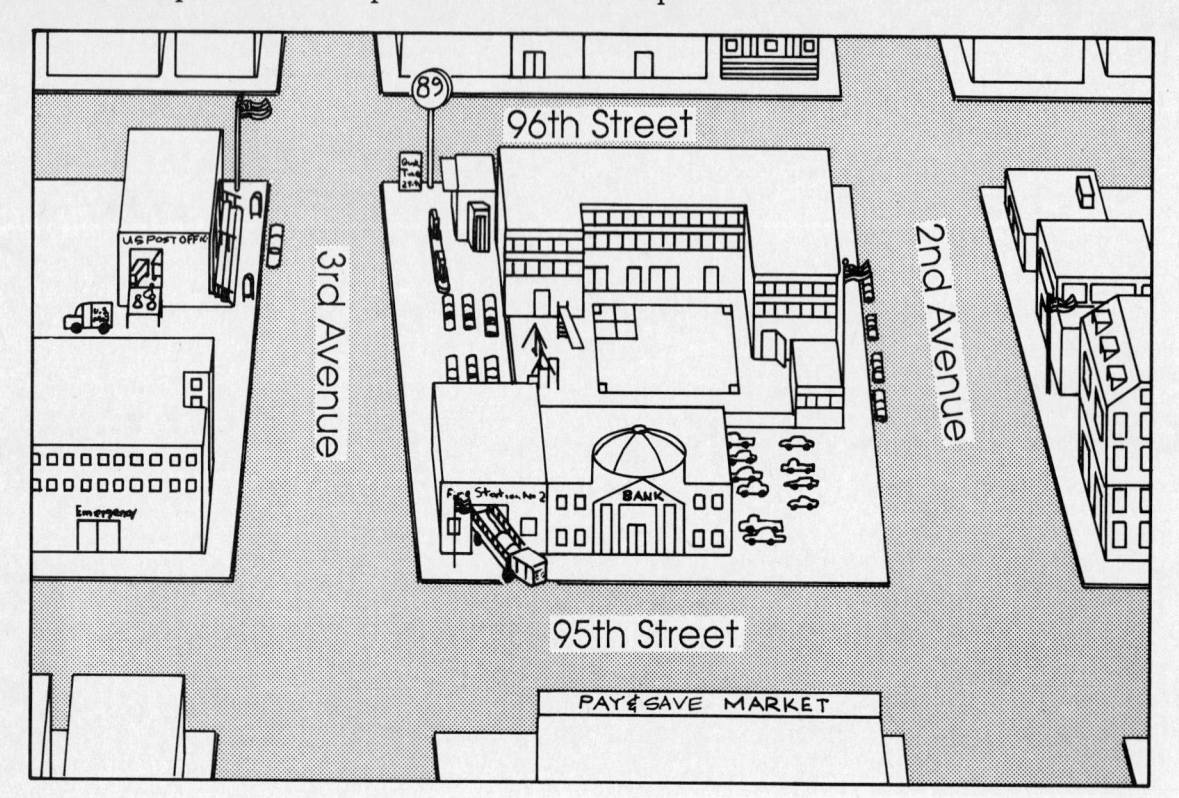

Reading a Map

Circle the right answers below.

1. Is the bank on 95th Street?   (Yes)   No

2. Is the post office on 3rd Avenue and 96th Street?   Yes   No

3. Is the school on 5th Avenue?   Yes   No

4. Is the gas station next to the firehouse?   Yes   No

5. Is the market between the school and the medical clinic?   Yes   No

What about You?

Write the phone numbers of these places in your community. Use the telephone book to help you. Work with a group.

1. School _____

2. Post Office _____

3. Police _____

4. Firehouse _____

42 / *Here to Stay in the USA*

Listen to This!

Your teacher will read the sentences below. Listen and circle the right answer in each box.

1. Marissa is going to the post office. It's on [15th / 50th] Street.

2. She's going to the medical clinic. It's on [North / South] Street.

3. She's going to the laundromat. It's on [30th / 33rd] Avenue.

4. She's going to the gas station. It's on [55th / 57th] Street and [7th / 5th] Avenue.

5. She's going to the bank. It's on [15th / 50th] Street and [49th / 94th] Avenue.

Conversation and Cooperation

Draw a map of your community. Include your apartment or house. Work with a group.

Your Community / 43

Community Talk

Read the dialogs below. Practice them with a classmate.

GRAND Ave / 17TH St.

— Where are you going?
— To the medical clinic.

— Excuse me. Where's the post office?
— It's on West Street.

— How do I get to the bank?
— Turn right. Go three blocks.

44 / *Here to Stay in the USA*

What's in the Picture?

An Emergency
Talk about the picture with your classmates and teacher.

EMERGENCY DIAL 911 FIRE POLICE MEDICAL

Student Space
Write your own words here.

Your Community / 45

Communication Strategies

> If you can't understand someone on the telephone, ask the person to **spell** the words you don't understand.

Please come to the medical clinic on Westerly Street.

Can you spell that, please?

Your appointment is with Dr. Huber.

Spell that name, please.

What is your name?

Guillermo Mendoza, G-U-I-L-L-E-R-M-O M-E-N-D-O-Z-A.

I don't understand you.

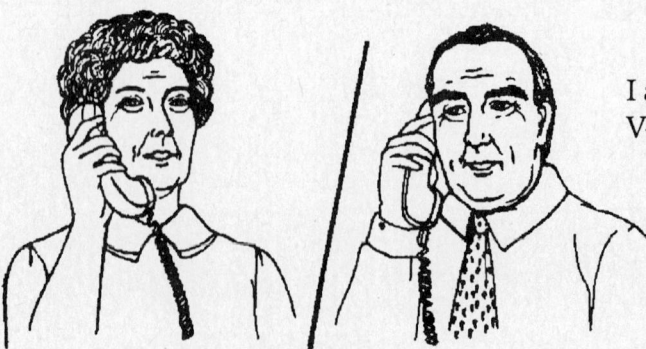

I am on Villamar Avenue. V-I-L-L-A-M-A-R.

46 / *Here to Stay in the USA*

Community Services

Every American community offers different services. Do you know where to find services in your community?

Look at the pictures. Write the correct word below each picture.

supermarket   medical clinic   library
garage   laundromat   post office

Where do you buy food?

1. *supermarket*

Where do you buy a money order?

2. _____

Where do you read a book?

3. _____

Where do you buy gas?

4. _____

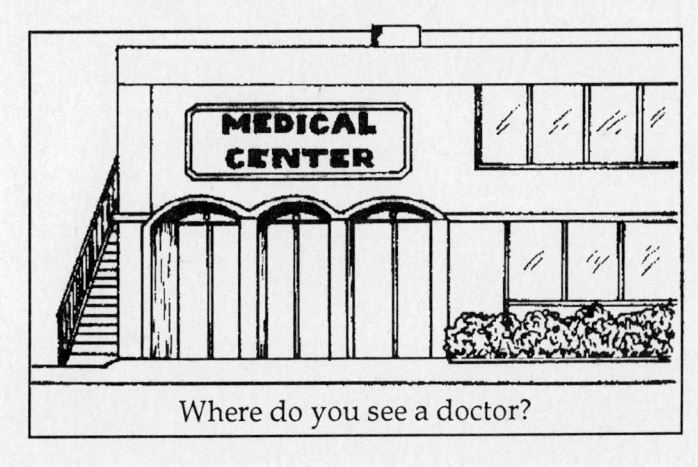

Where do you see a doctor?

5. _____

Where do you wash your clothes?

6. _____

Your Community / 47

Review Activity
Picture Story
Look at the pictures. Talk about the story in a group. Tell your story to the class.

48 / *Here to Stay in the USA*

UNIT FIVE

Shopping and Saving

Reading 1

In the Supermarket

Key Words and Phrases

| shopping | supermarket | soup | coffee |
| detergent | coupon | save | money |

1 Suzanna Ibarra is shopping in the supermarket.

2 She needs soup, coffee, and detergent.

3 She has a coupon for soup—she saves 25 cents.

MANUFACTURER COUPON   4/30/91
Save 25¢ when you buy 3 cans
25¢/3   25¢/3
Limit 1 coupon per package. Consumer must pay any sales tax.

4 She has a coupon for coffee—she saves 75 cents.

MANUFACTURER COUPON / EXPIRES MAY 1, 1991
Save 75¢
Limit 1 coupon per package. Consumer must pay any sales tax.
000053050

5 She has a coupon for detergent—she saves 50 cents.

Save 50¢   MANUFACTURER COUPON EXPIRES 4/1/91
50¢
Limit 1 coupon per package. Consumer must pay any sales tax.
79071

6 Suzanna saves a lot of money with coupons.

50 / *Here to Stay in the USA*

Reading 2

In the Department Store

Key Words and Phrases

| department store | shirt | socks | jeans |
| on sale | % off | buy | clothes |

1 Pablo Morales is shopping in a department store.

2 He needs a shirt, socks, and jeans.

3 The shirt is on sale—20% off.

4 The socks are on sale—15% off.

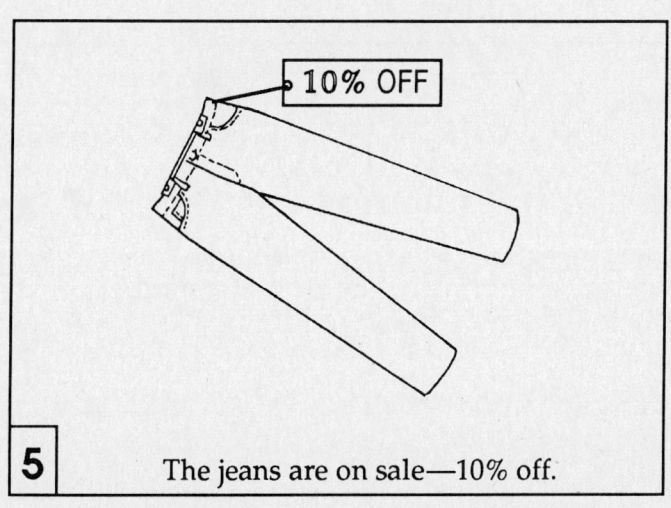

5 The jeans are on sale—10% off.

6 Pablo buys all of his clothes on sale.

Shopping and Saving / 51

Vocabulary Pictures
In the Supermarket

Look at the pictures below. Answer the questions at the bottom of the page.

Produce Section

| oranges | bananas | lettuce | carrots |

Dairy Section

| milk | cheese | butter | eggs |

Meat Section

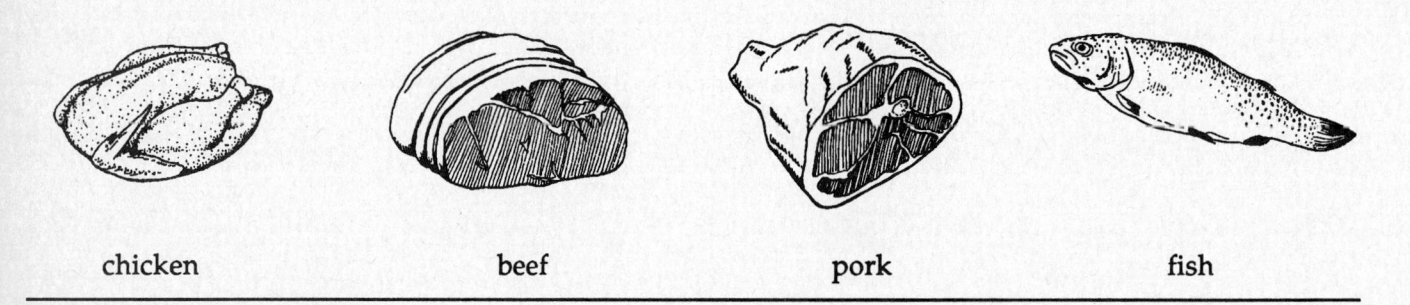

| chicken | beef | pork | fish |

Where Do You Find It?

Circle the right answer below.

1. Milk is in the   produce section.   (dairy section.)
2. Cheese is in the   dairy section.   meat section.
3. Beef is in the   meat section.   dairy section.
4. Bananas are in the   meat section.   produce section.
5. Chicken is in the   meat section.   dairy section.

52 / *Here to Stay in the USA*

Action Scripts
In the Department Store

Script 1 *Trying on Clothes*
(Materials: items pictured below or other articles of clothing)

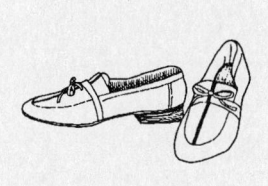

shoes    jacket 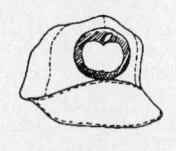   cap    T-shirt

1. Pick up the cap.
2. Try it on.
3. It doesn't fit. Take it off.
4. Try on the jacket.
5. It fits. Take it off.
6. Look at the price.
7. Put it down.

Script 2 *Buying Clothes*
(Materials: items pictured below or other articles of clothing)

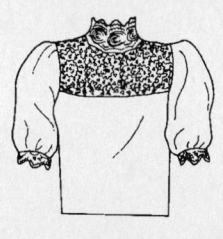

blouse 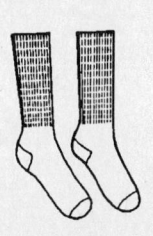   socks 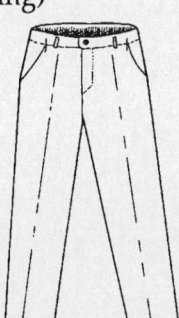   pants    sweater

1. Pick up the sweater.
2. Try it on.
3. It doesn't fit. Take it off.
4. Pick up the socks.
5. Look at the price.
6. Take them to the cashier.
7. Pay for them.

Shopping and Saving / 53

Discount Page

Read the ad below. Answer the questions at the bottom of the page.

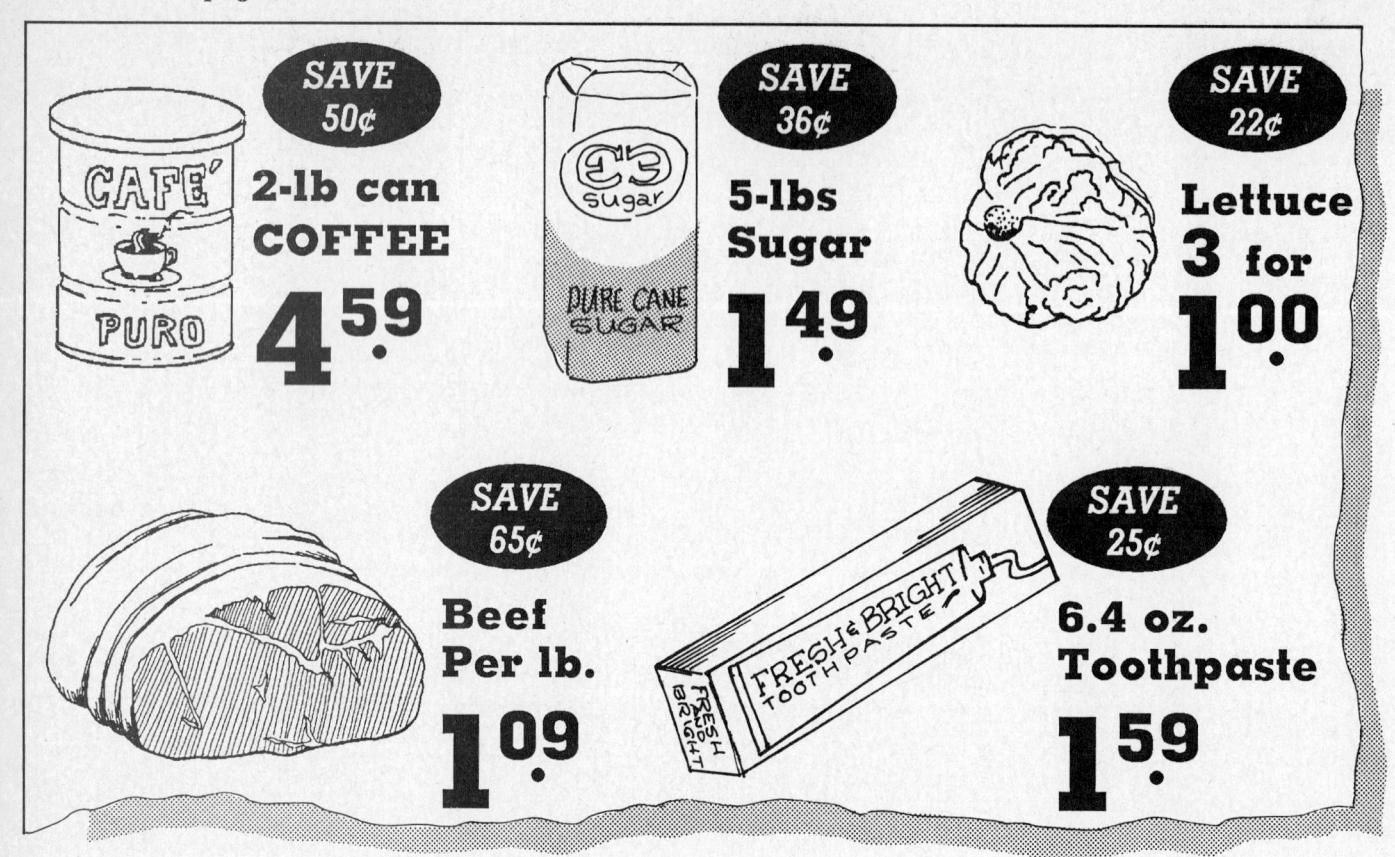

SAVE 50¢ — 2-lb can COFFEE — 4.59

SAVE 36¢ — 5-lbs Sugar — 1.49

SAVE 22¢ — Lettuce 3 for 1.00

SAVE 65¢ — Beef Per lb. — 1.09

SAVE 25¢ — 6.4 oz. Toothpaste — 1.59

Reading Discount Ads

Write the answers on the lines below.

1. How much do you save on coffee? __50¢__
2. How much do you save on beef? _____
3. How much do you save on toothpaste? _____
4. How much do you save on sugar? _____
5. How much do you save on lettuce? _____

What about You?

Name four places to buy food in your neighborhood. Write the price of one food item at each store.

	Store	Food	Price
1.			
2.			
3.			
4.			

Here to Stay in the USA

Listen to This!

Your teacher will read the sentences below. Listen and circle the right answer in the boxes.

Oscar Gomez is shopping in the supermarket.

He goes to the **meat section**.

1. Ham is [$2.99 / $3.99] a pound.

2. Fish is [$2.98 / $2.89] a pound.

He goes to the **produce section**.

3. Tomatoes are [59 / 69] cents a pound.

4. Apples are [79 / 69] cents a pound.

Now he goes to the **dairy section**.

5. Ice cream is [$1.50 / $1.59] a pint.

6. Milk is [$1.89 / $1.99] a gallon.

Conversation and Cooperation

Make up a shopping list with your classmates. What will you buy? How much will it cost?

Food Items	Cost
_____	_____
_____	_____
_____	_____
_____	_____
	Total Cost $ _____

Shopping and Saving / 55

Shopping Talk

Read the dialogs below. Practice them with a classmate.

- I like your shirt. Where did you buy it?
- At Merlin's. It was on sale.

50% OFF

- How do you like this shirt?
- It's nice, but too expensive!

- Excuse me, is this on sale?
- Yes, it's 50% off.

- What did you buy?
- I bought a coat.

20% OFF

CLEARANCE SALE

56 / *Here to Stay in the USA*

What's in the Picture?

At the Supermarket
Talk about the picture with your classmates and teacher.

Student Space
Write your own words here.

Shopping and Saving / 57

Communication Strategies

> When you get a bill or receipt, **check it** for mistakes. Make sure it's correct.

Hello, may I help you? — Yes, I have a question about my bill.

Yes, can I help you? — I think my bill is wrong.

Is there a problem? — Yes, would you add this again, please?

What can I do for you? — Would you please add this again?

58 / *Here to Stay in the USA*

Receipts and Bills

When you buy something you get a receipt or a bill. The receipt or bill tells you what you bought, how much it costs, and the sales tax. Read the receipts and the bill below. Write the answers to the questions.

```
         WALDEN FOOD MARKET
         BREAD              1.29
         CARROTS             .59
  2.5LB @ .59/LB
         POTATOES           1.21
         TEA                2.69
  3.51LB @ .49/LB
         BANANAS             .82
         LOWFAT MILK        1.68
  2LB @ .69/LB
         APPLES             1.14
              TOTAL         9.42
              CASH         10.00
              CHANGE         .58
      THANK YOU FOR SHOPPING AT
              WALDEN'S!
```

Supermarket Receipt

1. How much is the bread? $1.29
2. How much is the tea? _____
3. How much is the milk? _____
4. How much are the apples? _____
5. How much do you pay? _____

```
jb department store   CUSTOMER'S RECEIPT

SALESPERSON  TYPE  TRANS  STORE   DATE
990034        6    0777   07711  FEB1090

DEPT/CLASS                      AMOUNT
MENS SHIRT                       20.00
MENS PANTS                       32.00
MENS SOCKS                        1.50
              SUBTOTAL           53.50
              TAX                 3.75
              CASH               57.25
```

Department Store Receipt

1. How much is the shirt? _____
2. How much is the subtotal? _____
3. How much is the tax? _____
4. How much do you pay? _____
5. What is the date? _____

```
          GUEST CHECK
      SERVER 150  TABLE 101/1

  SOUP                   1.75
  SALAD                  1.95
  HAMBURGER              4.75
  FRENCH FRIES            .75
  ICE CREAM               .95
  COFFEE                  .65
                        ------
          TOTAL          10.80
          TAX             .75
                        ------
          GRAND TOTAL   11.55

    THANK YOU-FRAYER'S CAFE
    PLEASE PAY YOUR SERVER
```

Restaurant Bill

1. How much is the soup? _____
2. How much is the hamburger? _____
3. How much is the subtotal? _____
4. How much is the tax? _____
5. How much do you pay? _____

Shopping and Saving / 59

Money Review Activity

Coins

penny—$.01

nickel—$.05

dime—$.10

quarter—$.25

Bills

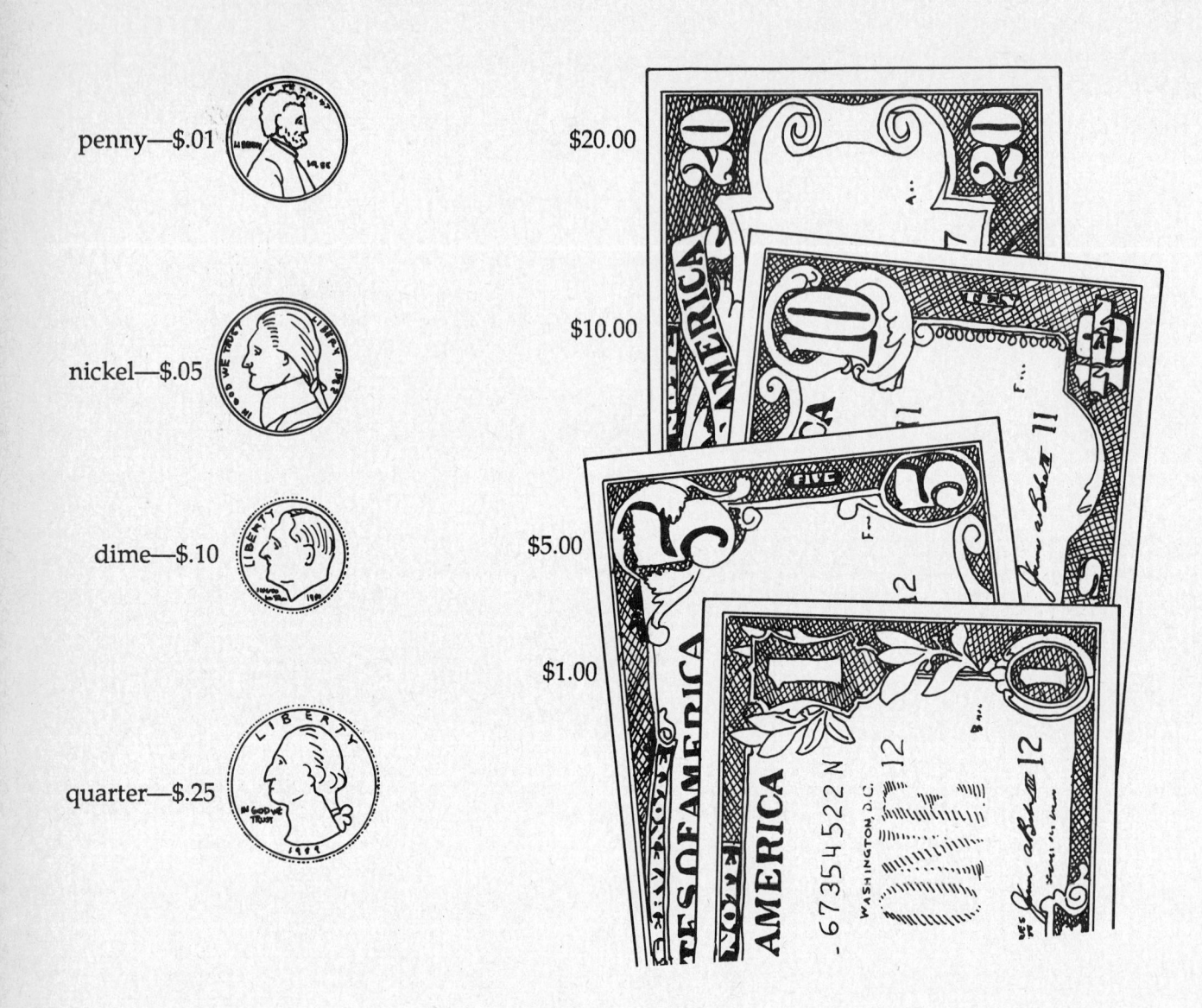

$20.00

$10.00

$5.00

$1.00

How Much Is It?

Add up each amount. Write the totals on the lines.

1. One dime, three nickels, and a five-dollar bill = _____

2. Two quarters, four dimes, and one nickel = _____

3. Two twenty-dollar bills = _____

4. One twenty-dollar bill, two quarters, and one penny = _____

5. Five dimes, five nickels, and five pennies = _____

60 / *Here to Stay in the USA*

UNIT SIX
Working in America

Employee	Hourly	Gross Weekly Earnings
P. Morales	7.50	300.00

Deductions			
F.I.C.A.*	Federal WIT*	State W/T	Net Pay
22.53	40.00	6.00	231.47

61

Reading 1

Different Jobs

Key Words and Phrases

| work | drive | truck | hairdresser |
| cashier | owns | restaurant | boss |

1. Pablo, Suzanna, Elena, and Miguel work in Dallas.
2. Pablo Morales drives a truck. 
3. Suzanna is a hairdresser. 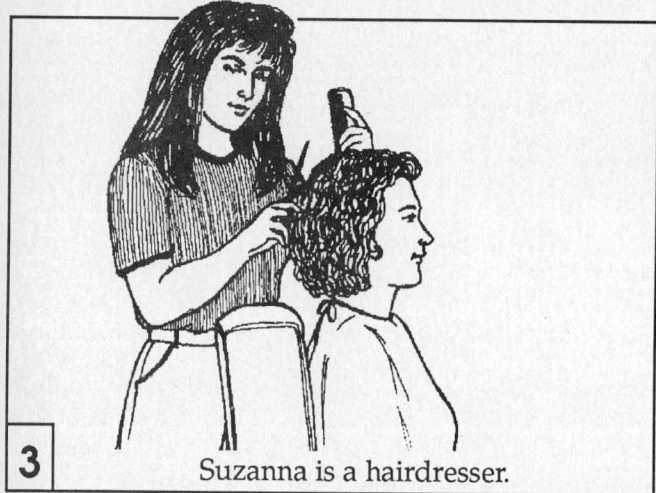
4. Elena Martinez is a cashier. 
5. Miguel Ochoa owns a restaurant. 
6. He is the boss. 

62 / *Here to Stay in the USA*

Reading 2

Payday

Key Words and Phrases

today	payday	hours	a week
an hour	makes	government	keeps

1. Today is payday for Pablo Morales.

2. He works 40 hours a week.

3. He makes $7.50 an hour.

NAME	HOURLY RATE		
P. Morales	7	5	0
J. Sanchez	7	0	0
Louis Kammer	7	5	0
Keith Hernandez	7	0	0
Hung Van Nguyen	7	0	0

4. He makes $300.00 a week.

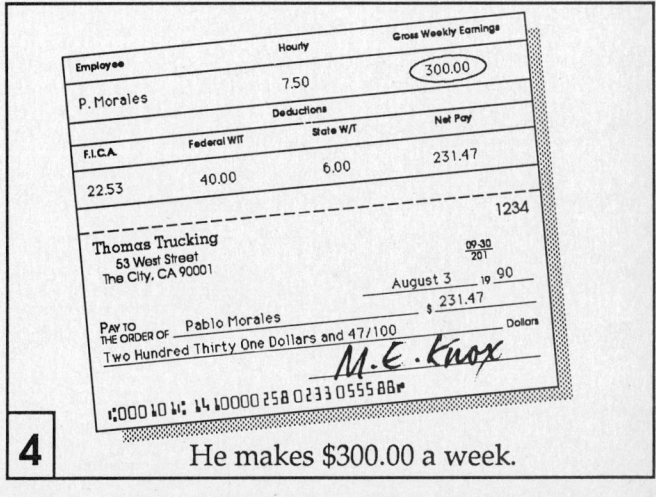

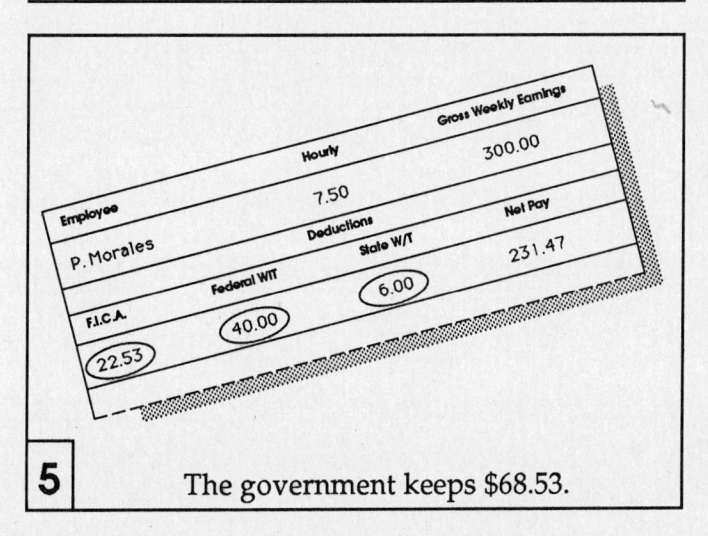

5. The government keeps $68.53.

6. Pablo keeps $231.47.

Working in America / 63

Vocabulary Pictures
Jobs

Write the correct letter under each picture.
- a. computer operator
- b. farm worker
- c. waiter
- d. mechanic
- e. bus driver
- f. cashier

1. e
2. ___ 
3. ___ 
4. ___ 
5. ___ 
6. ___ 

64 / *Here to Stay in the USA*

Action Scripts
On the Job

Script 1 *Carpenter*
(Materials: hammer, nails, ruler, small piece of wood, screwdriver, screws.)

1. You're a carpenter.
2. Pick up a hammer.
3. Pick up two nails.
4. Hammer the nails into a piece of wood.
5. Pick up a ruler.
6. Measure the wood. How long is it?
7. Pick up a screwdriver.
8. Pick up a screw.
9. Screw it into the wood.
10. Put the screwdriver down.

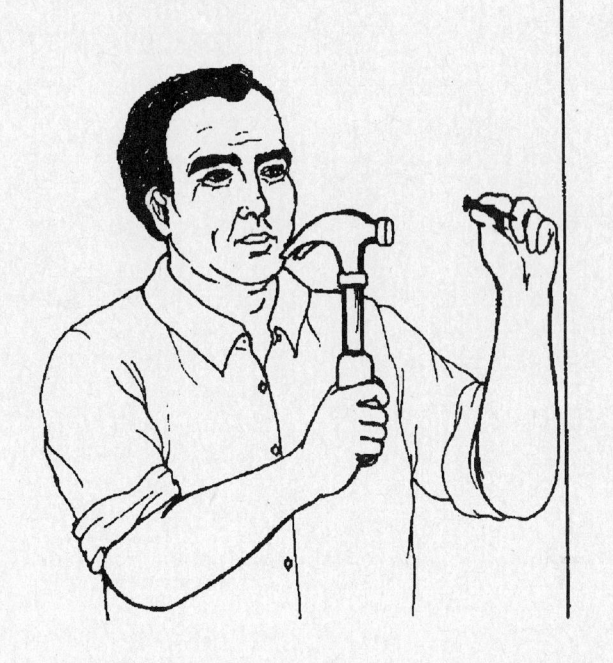

Script 2 *Cashier*
(Materials: one ten-dollar bill, three five-dollar bills, ten one-dollar bills, seven quarters, five dimes, five nickels, ten pennies. Use real or play money.)

1. You're a cashier.
2. Open the cash register.
3. Count your money. How much do you have?
4. Count it again.
5. A customer's bill is $5.03. He gives you $10.00. Make change.
6. A customer's bill is $1.14. She gives you $5.00. Make change.
7. A customer's bill is $2.64. She gives you $5.00. Make change.
8. Count all your money.
9. Count it again.
10. Close the register.

Working in America / 65

Work Schedule

Look at the work schedule below. Answer the questions under the schedule.

Davis Dry Cleaners						
	M	T	W	TH	F	S
Juan	10–6	10–6	10–6	off	10–6	10–6
Thomas	3–6	3–6	3–6	3–6	3–6	10–6
Mary	10–6	10–6	10–6	10–6	10–6	off

Reading a Schedule

Circle the right answers below.

1. How many days does Juan work?   3 days   (5 days)
2. When is Mary off?   Saturday   Tuesday
3. How many hours does Juan work on Friday?   4 hours   8 hours
4. When does Thomas come to work on Monday?   3:00   10:00
5. How many hours does Mary work each week?   40 hours   30 hours

What about You?

Write about yourself on the lines below.

1. Where do you work? _____
2. How many days do you work? _____
3. What are your hours? _____
4. Are you full-time or part-time? _____
5. Do you like your job? _____

66 / *Here to Stay in the USA*

Listen to This!

Your teacher will read the sentences below. Listen and circle the right answer in each box.

1. David Lee is a [bus / truck] driver.

2. He makes [$8.00 / $18.00] an hour.

3. He works [40 / 14] hours a week.

4. He has [Fridays / Saturdays] off.

5. Maria Lopez is a [farm worker / farmer].

6. She makes [$5.50 / $5.25] an hour.

7. She works [40 / 30] hours a week.

8. She has [Saturdays / Sundays] off.

Conversation and Cooperation

Talk to three different people in your class. Ask them their occupation, and the days and the hours they work.

	Name	Occupation	Days	Hours
1.				
2.				
3.				

Working in America / 67

Job Talk

Read the dialogs below. Practice them with a classmate.

- Do you work on Sunday?
- No, it's my day off.

- How's the pay?
- I make minimum wage—$3.35 an hour.

- Do you have a job?
- Yeah, at Lenny's Restaurant.

- What time do you go to work?
- At 3:00. I get off at 11:00.

68 / *Here to Stay in the USA*

What's in the Picture?

Payday

Talk about the picture with your classmates and teacher.

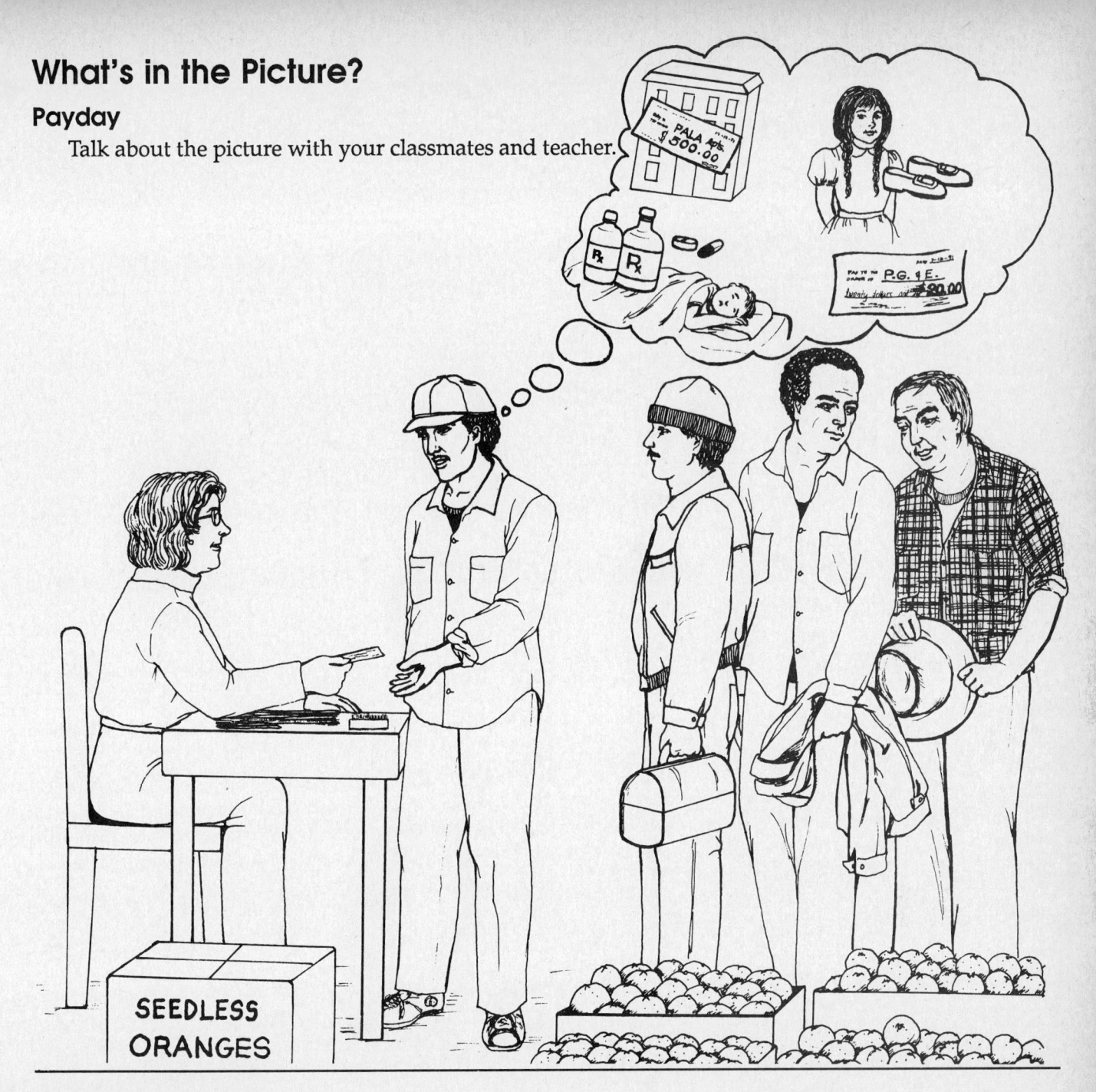

Student Space

Write your own words here.

Working in America / 69

Communication Strategies

> If you don't understand what people at work are saying tell them **"I don't understand."**

Take these to the delivery desk.

I'm sorry, I don't understand.

Be here tomorrow at noon.

I don't understand. Could you say that again?

Drive this order to 3rd Avenue and 33rd Street.

Excuse me, I don't understand.

You'll make $5.00 an hour, eight hours a day.

Please say that again.

Your Paycheck and Paycheck Stub

Americans must pay income taxes. The government keeps part of your paycheck. Your taxes pay for schools, roads, and hospitals.

Read the paycheck and paycheck stub below, then answer the questions.

Paycheck Stub

Employee	Hourly	Gross Weekly Earnings
P. Morales	7.50	300.00

Deductions			
F.I.C.A.	Federal WIT	State W/T*	Net Pay
22.53	40.00	6.00	231.47

*Withholding amounts vary from state to state.

Paycheck

Thomas Trucking 1234
53 West Street
The City, CA 90001

09-30 / 201

August 3, 19 90

PAY TO THE ORDER OF __Pablo Morales__ $ 231.47

__Two Hundred Thirty One Dollars and 47/100__ Dollars

City Bank
672 North Ave
The City, CA 90001

M.E. Knox

⑈000 10 ⑈: 14 10000 258 0233 0555 88 ⑈

Wages and Taxes

Write the answers on the lines below.

1. Whose paycheck is this? __Pablo Morales__

2. What is the date on the check? _____

3. How much does she make an hour? _____

4. How much does she make before taxes? _____

5. How much does she make after taxes? _____

Working in America / 71

Review Activity

Look at the words and pictures below. Write the name of the job under the right picture.

computer operator   waiter   bus driver
farm worker   mechanic   cashier

1. _____

2. _____

3. _____

4. _____

5. _____

6. _____

72 / *Here to Stay in the USA*

UNIT SEVEN

Finding a Job

Reading 1

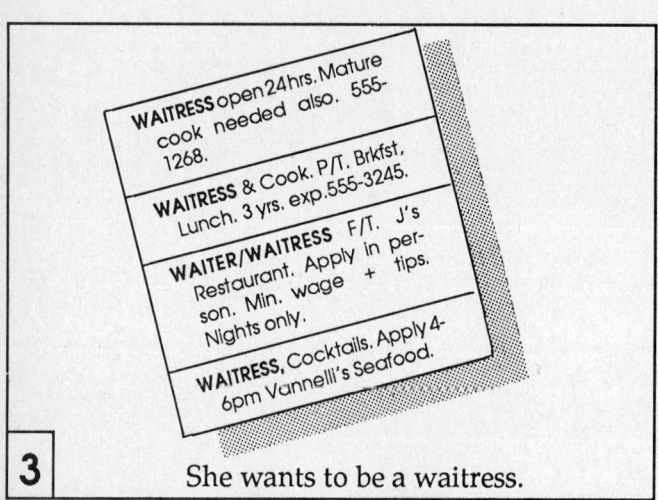

Looking for a Job

Key Words and Phrases

| is looking | job | want | waitress | has |
| experience | call | restaurants | fill out | application |

1. Her name is Dolores Mendoza.
2. She is looking for a job.
3. She wants to be a waitress.
4. She has experience.
5. She calls restaurants.
6. She fills out applications.

74 / *Here to Stay in the USA*

Reading 2

The Interview

Key Words and Phrases

interview   answering questions   asking questions
salary   hours   benefits

1. Dolores has an interview today.
2. She is answering questions about herself. 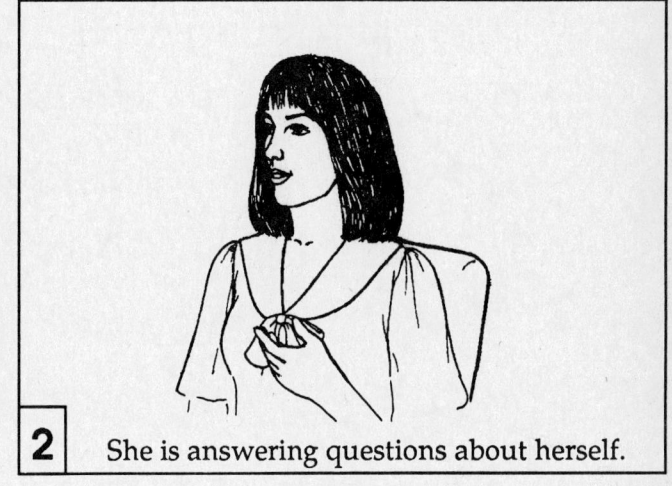
3. She is asking questions about the job. 
4. "What is the salary?" 
5. "What are the hours?" 
6. "What are the benefits?" 

Finding a Job / 75

Vocabulary Pictures

Application Form

Read the application form below. Answer the questions under the form.

APPLICATION FOR EMPLOYMENT

Name: **Dolores** (First) **T.** (Middle Int.) **Mendoza** (Last)

Social Security Number: **987/65/4322**

Address: **182 Grand St.** (Street) **#29** (Apt.) **New York** (City) **NY** (State) **11432** (Zip)

Marital Status: ☑ Single ☐ Married ☐ Divorced

Phone: **(212) 555-3036**

Position you are applying for: **Waitress**

Date available for work: **immediately**   ☑ Full Time ☐ Part Time

Do you have transportation to work? ☑ YES ☐ NO

Are you a United States Citizen or do you have a work visa? ☑ YES ☐ NO   If not, type of visa _____

WORK EXPERIENCE
List below your two most recent employers, beginning with the current or most recent one.

Name: **El Paso Cafe**   Address: **24 Broom St., El Paso, TX**
Job Title: **Waitress**   Name of Supervisor: **Mrs. Mendez**   Phone: **(915) 555-0110**
Date started: **12/83** (Mo/Yr)   Date left: **3/88** (Mo/Yr)   Salary $ **4.00 per hr. + tips**

Name: **Star Cafe**   Address: **1335 99th Ave., El Paso, TX**
Job Title: **Waitress**   Name of Supervisor: **Mr. Hopson**   Phone: **(915) 555-3026**
Date started: **4/81** (Mo/Yr)   Date left: **11/83** (Mo/Yr)   Salary $ **3.50 per hr + tips**

Signature: *Delores Mendoza*   Date: **7/15/89**

Application Questions

Write the answers on the lines below.

1. Who is applying for a job? **Dolores T. Mendoza**

2. What job is she applying for? _____

3. Does she have experience? _____

4. What is her social security number? _____

5. Does she want full-time or part-time work? _____

76 / *Here to Stay in the USA*

Action Scripts
Applying for a Job

Script 1 *Introduce Yourself*
(Materials: application form, pen, someone to role-play as manager)

1. Stand up.
2. Walk to the door.
3. Knock on the door.
4. Shake hands with the manager.
5. Introduce yourself.

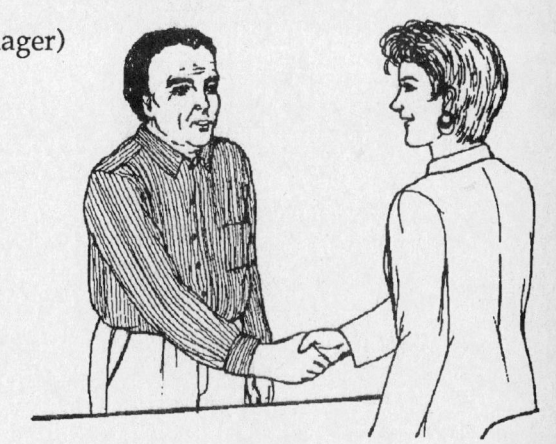

Script 2 *Filling Out an Application*
(Materials: application form, pen, someone to role-play as manager)

1. Sit down.
2. Pick up an application form.
3. Write your last name.
4. Write your first name.
5. Write today's date.

Script 3 *Personal Information*
(Materials: application form, pen, someone to role-play as manager)

1. Write your date of birth.
2. Write your social security number.
3. Write your telephone number.
4. Write your marital status.
5. Write the name of the job you are applying for.

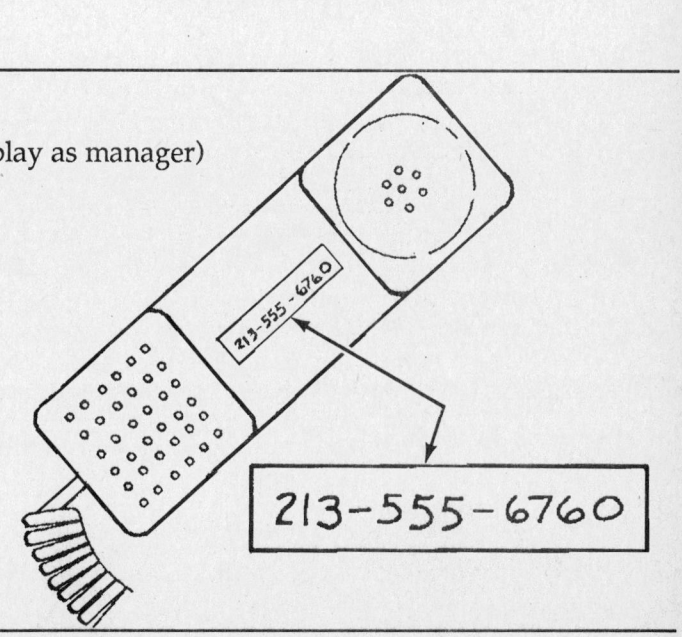

Finding a Job / 77

The Want Ads

Read the want ads. Answer the questions under the ads.

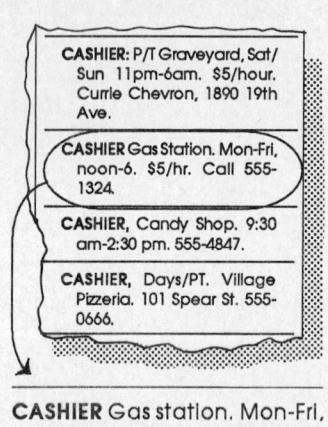

CASHIER Gas station. Mon-Fri, noon-6. $5/hr. Call 555-1324.

TRUCK DRIVER P/T Exp'd pref. Tu-Fri, 10-6. Dave 555-1279. $7/hr.

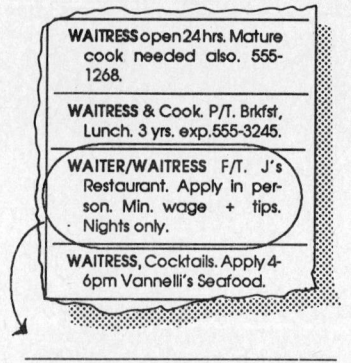

WAITER/WAITRESS F/T. J's Restaurant. Apply in person. Min. wage + tips. Nights only.

Reading Want Ads

Put a check (✓) in the right box below.

1. The truck driver job pays $7.00 an hour.   ☑ Yes ☐ No
2. The truck driver works on Monday night.   ☐ Yes ☐ No
3. The waiter/waitress job is full-time.   ☐ Yes ☐ No
4. The cashier job pays $5.00 an hour.   ☐ Yes ☐ No
5. The cashier works Monday through Friday.   ☐ Yes ☐ No

What about You?

Put a check (✓) in the box that tells about your work experience.

Do you have experience

1. driving a truck?   ☐ Yes ☐ No
2. working with machines?   ☐ Yes ☐ No
3. caring for children?   ☐ Yes ☐ No
4. caring for sick people?   ☐ Yes ☐ No
5. cooking?   ☐ Yes ☐ No
6. picking fruit?   ☐ Yes ☐ No
7. canning fruit?   ☐ Yes ☐ No
8. waiting tables?   ☐ Yes ☐ No
9. building houses?   ☐ Yes ☐ No
10. working in a hotel?   ☐ Yes ☐ No

Listen to This!

Your teacher will read the sentences below. Listen and circle the right answer in each box.

1. This job is for a | waiter. / driver. |

2. The salary is | $5.00 / $8.00 | an hour.

3. You work | nights. / days. |

4. The work is | full-time. / part-time. |

5. You work | Mondays and Wednesdays. / Monday through Friday. |

Conversation and Cooperation

Work with a group. Write three questions you will ask on your job interview.

1. _____

2. _____

3. _____

Finding a Job / 79

Interview Talk

Read the dialogs below. Practice them with a classmate.

- We'll call you next week.
- Thanks.

- What was your last job?
- I picked apples in Washington.

- What skills do you have?
- I can fix TVs and radios.

- Do you have experience?
- Yes, I drove a truck in San Antonio.

80 / *Here to Stay in the USA*

What's in the Picture?
Looking for a Job
Talk about the picture with your classmates and teacher.

Miguel's Restaurant

HELP WANTED
We hire only US Citizens and Lawfully Authorized Alien Workers

MENU   MENU

Student Space
Write your own words here.

Finding a Job / 81

Communication Strategies

> In a job interview, ask **questions**. Find out about the job.

The pay is good. — Are there benefits?

We need an assistant manager. — What are the duties?

Do you have any questions? — What are the hours?

Can you work overtime? — Yes, how often?

82 / Here to Stay in the USA

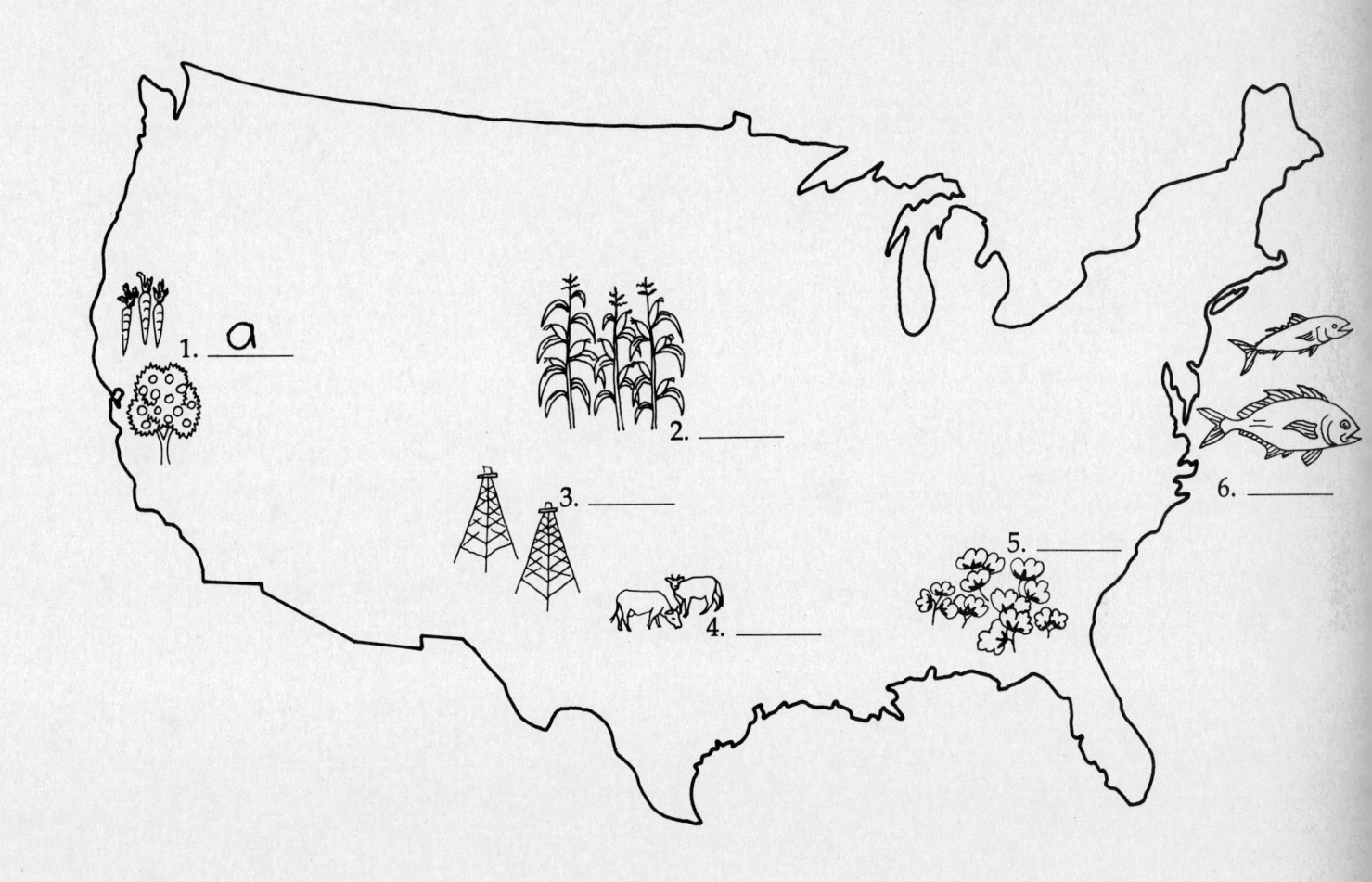

American Products

American products come from all over America. Write the product letter in the correct place on the map.

- a. fruits and vegetables
- b. oil
- c. cotton
- d. fish
- e. cattle
- f. corn

1. a
2. _____
3. _____
4. _____
5. _____
6. _____

Finding a Job / 83

Review Activity

Fill out this job application with information about yourself.

APPLICATION FOR EMPLOYMENT

Social Security Number _____ / _____ / _____

Name _____
      First   Middle Int.   Last

Address _____
      Street   Apt.   City   State   Zip

Marital Status ☐ Single ☐ Married ☐ Divorced   Phone _____

Position you are applying for _____

Date available for work _____ ☐ Full Time ☐ Part Time

Do you have transportation to work? ☐ YES ☐ NO

Are you a United States Citizen or do you have a work visa? ☐ YES ☐ NO   If not, type of visa _____

WORK EXPERIENCE

List below your two most recent employers, beginning with the current or most recent one.

Name _____ Address _____

Job Title _____ Name of Supervisor _____ Phone _____

Date started _____ Date left _____ Salary $ _____
            Mo/Yr   Mo/Yr

Name _____ Address _____

Job Title _____ Name of Supervisor _____ Phone _____

Date started _____ Date left _____ Salary $ _____
            Mo/Yr   Mo/Yr

_____   _____
         Signature   Date

UNIT EIGHT

Housing

Reading 1

The Apartment

Key Words and Phrases

apartment	rooms	cook	kitchen
sleep	bedroom	living room	rent

1. José and Elena Martinez live in an apartment building.

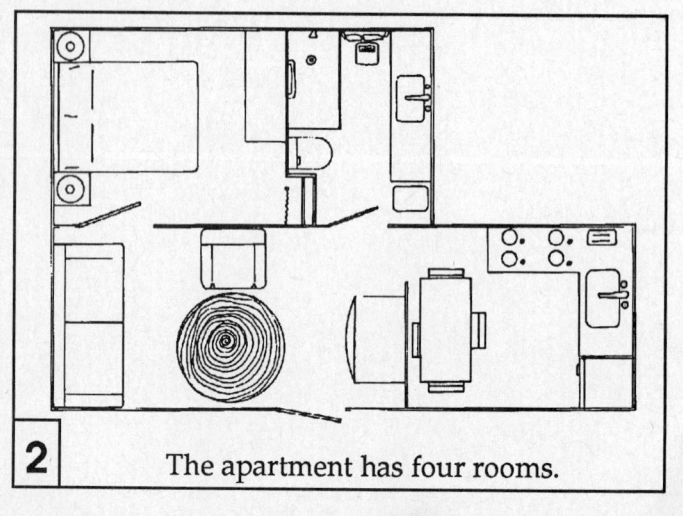

2. The apartment has four rooms.

3. José and Elena cook in the kitchen.

4. They sleep in the bedroom.

5. They watch TV in the living room.

6. The rent is $590.00 a month.

Reading 2

Apartment Problems

Key Words and Phrases

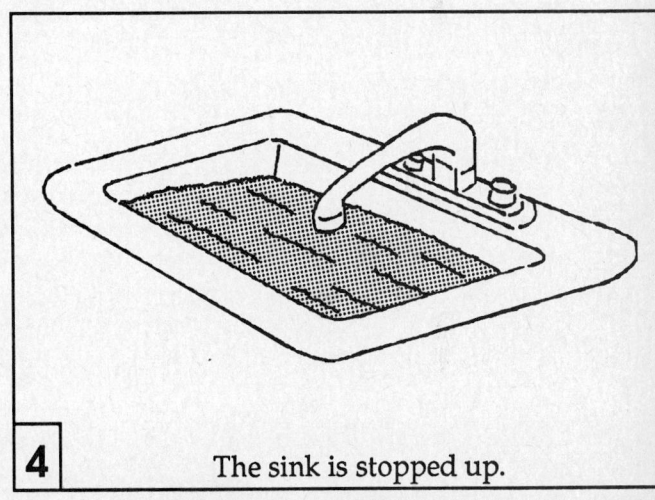

problems	roof	leak	bathroom
lock	door	broken	sink
stopped up	call	manager	fix

1 José and Elena have problems with the apartment.

2 The roof leaks in the bathroom.

3 The lock on the door is broken.

4 The sink is stopped up.

5 They call the manager.

6 The manager fixes the lock.

Housing / 87

Vocabulary Pictures
The Apartment
Look at the pictures below. Answer the questions under the pictures.

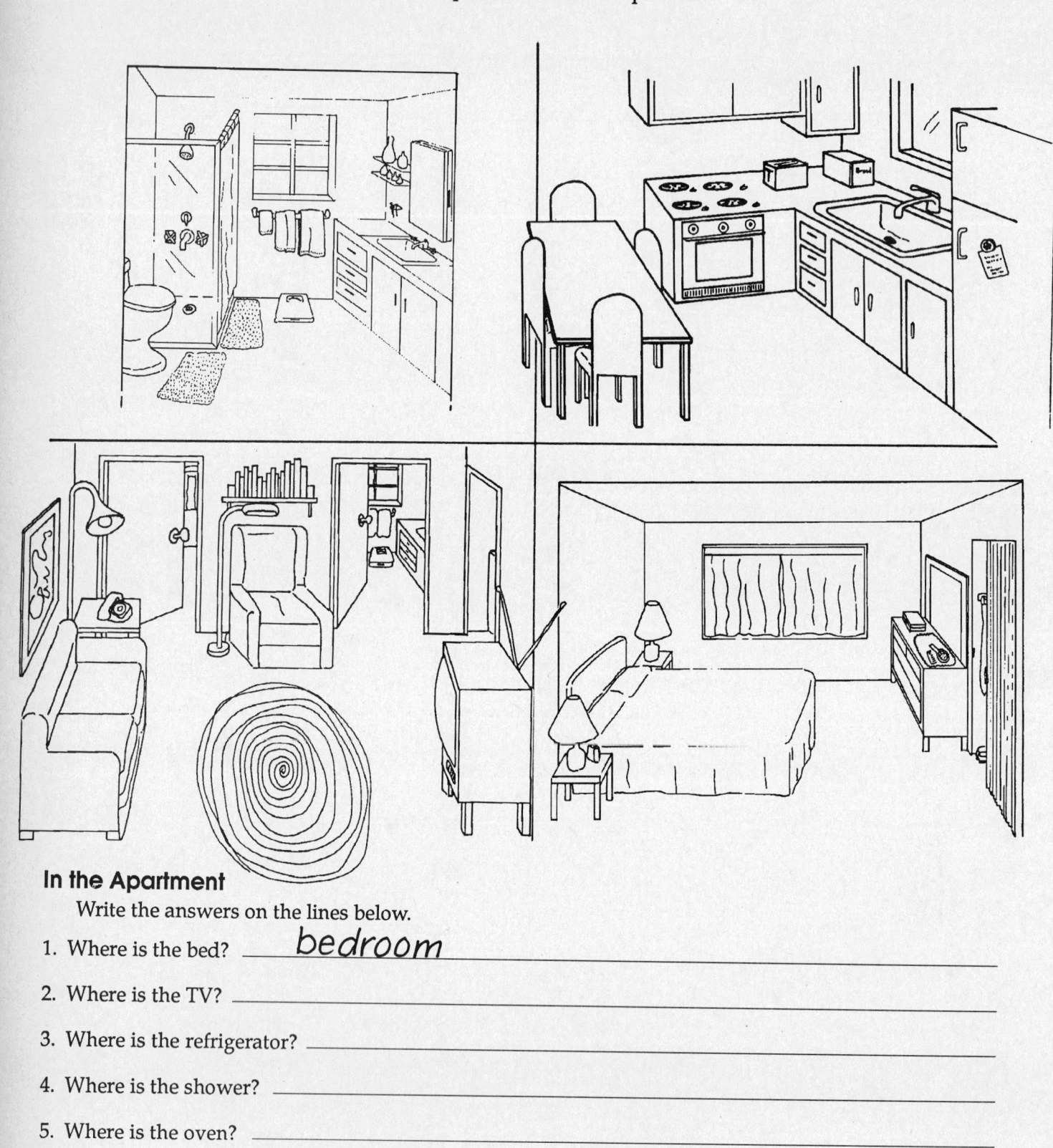

In the Apartment
Write the answers on the lines below.

1. Where is the bed? __bedroom__

2. Where is the TV? _____

3. Where is the refrigerator? _____

4. Where is the shower? _____

5. Where is the oven? _____

88 / *Here to Stay in the USA*

Action Scripts
In the House

Script 1 *The Kitchen*
(Materials: set up room as kitchen—refrigerator, sink, dishes, dishcloth)

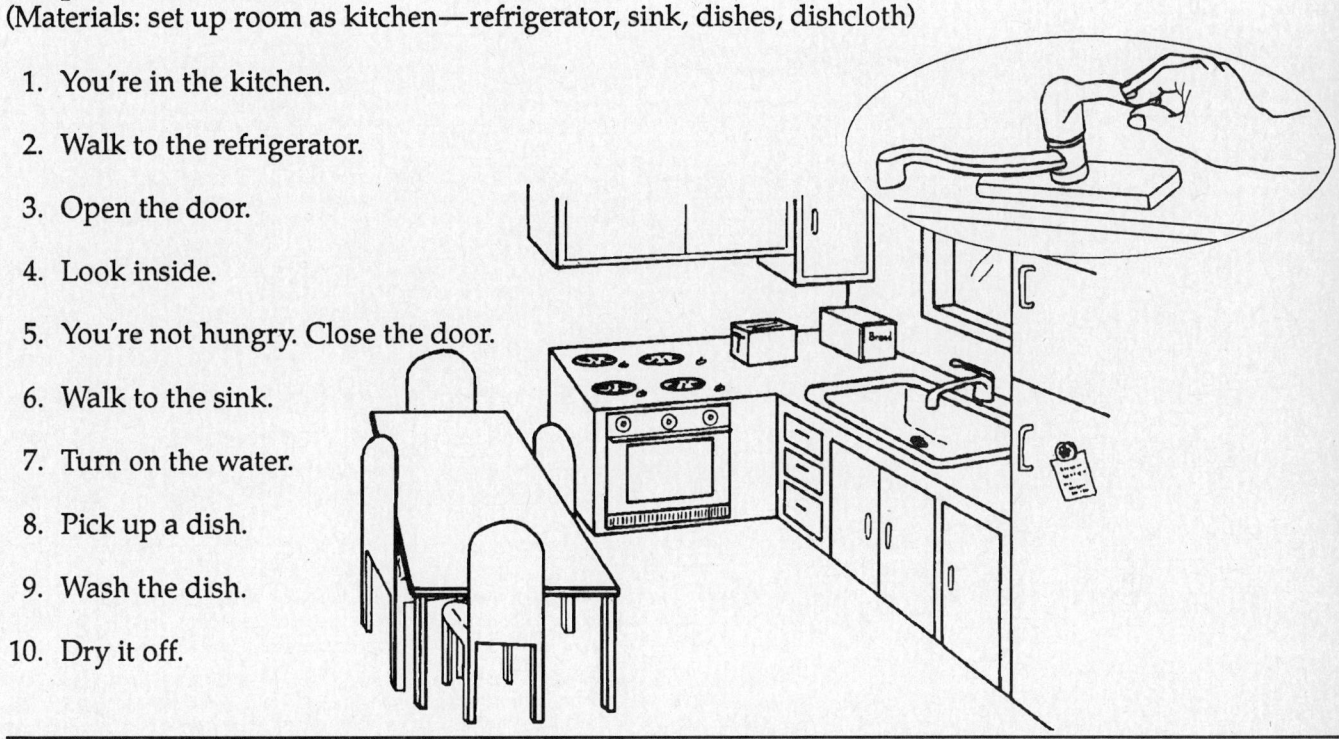

1. You're in the kitchen.
2. Walk to the refrigerator.
3. Open the door.
4. Look inside.
5. You're not hungry. Close the door.
6. Walk to the sink.
7. Turn on the water.
8. Pick up a dish.
9. Wash the dish.
10. Dry it off.

Script 2 *The Bathroom*
(Materials: set up room as bathroom—sink, faucet, soap, scale)

1. You're in the bathroom.
2. Walk to the sink.
3. Turn on the faucet.
4. Turn on the hot water.
5. Turn on the cold water.
6. Pick up the soap.
7. Wash your hands.
8. Dry your hands.
9. Step on the scale.
10. Step off the scale.

Housing / 89

For Rent

Read the rent ads below. Answer the questions under the ads.

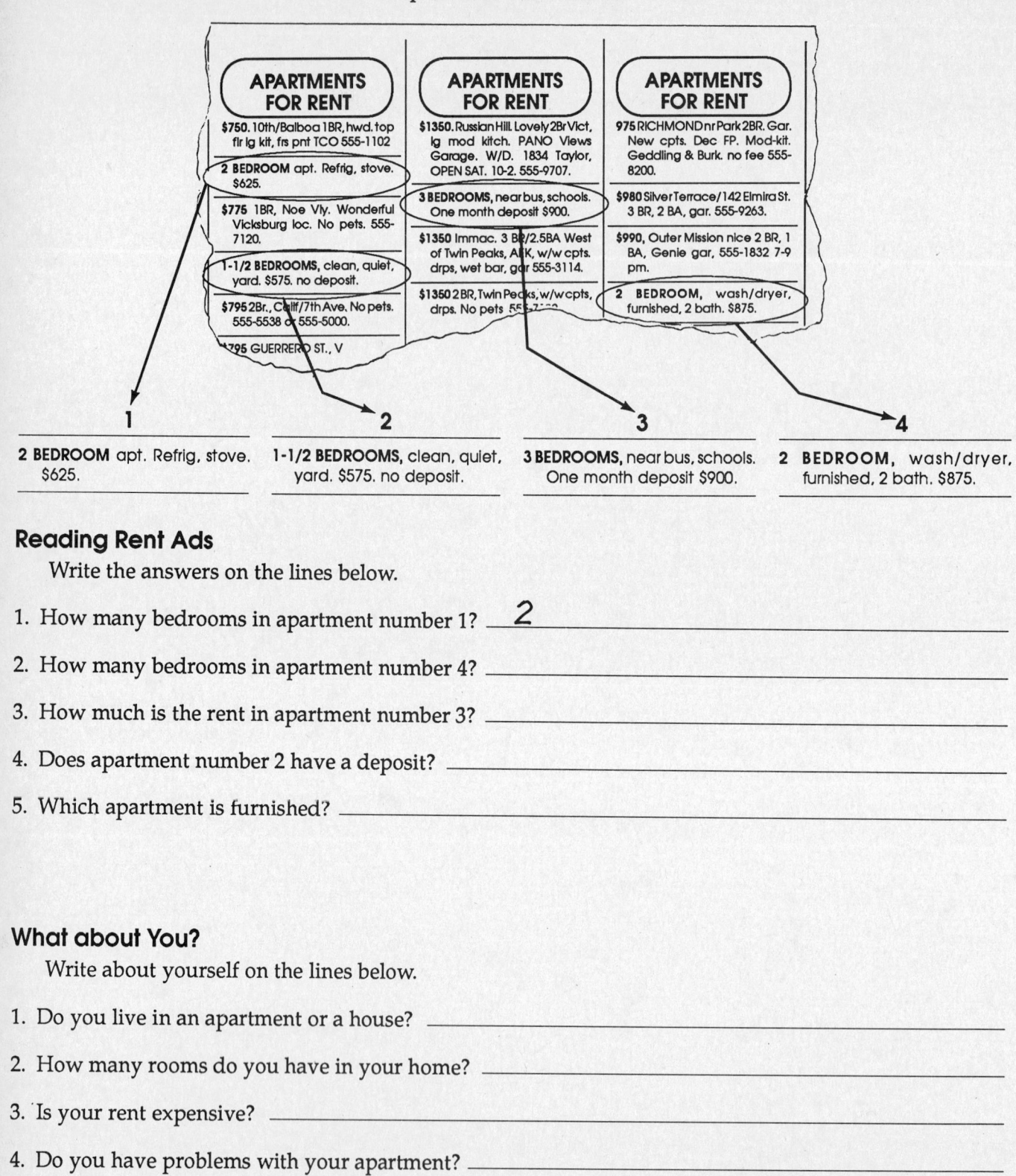

1. 2 BEDROOM apt. Refrig, stove. $625.

2. 1-1/2 BEDROOMS, clean, quiet, yard. $575. no deposit.

3. 3 BEDROOMS, near bus, schools. One month deposit $900.

4. 2 BEDROOM, wash/dryer, furnished, 2 bath. $875.

Reading Rent Ads

Write the answers on the lines below.

1. How many bedrooms in apartment number 1? __2__

2. How many bedrooms in apartment number 4? _____

3. How much is the rent in apartment number 3? _____

4. Does apartment number 2 have a deposit? _____

5. Which apartment is furnished? _____

What about You?

Write about yourself on the lines below.

1. Do you live in an apartment or a house? _____

2. How many rooms do you have in your home? _____

3. Is your rent expensive? _____

4. Do you have problems with your apartment? _____

5. What is your landlord's name? _____

Listen to This!

Your teacher will read the sentences below. Listen and circle the right answer in each box.

Marissa Espinosa is looking for an apartment.

1. This apartment has [three / two] bedrooms.

2. It's near the [school. / bus station.]

3. The rent is [$400.00 / $440.00] a month.

4. The apartment is [furnished. / unfurnished.]

Puri Mendiola is looking for an apartment.

1. This apartment has [one / three] bedrooms.

2. It's [a furnished / an unfurnished] apartment.

3. The rent is [$630.00 / $713.00] a month.

4. You need a [one / two] month deposit.

Conversation and Cooperation

Ask three people in your class about their apartments or houses.

Name	Address	How Many Bedrooms?
1.		
2.		
3.		

Housing / 91

Housing Talk

Read the dialogs below. Practice them with a classmate.

- How's your new apartment?
- Good. The rent is cheap.
- How's your apartment?
- Too small. It's crowded.
- Do you live in an apartment?
- No, my wife and I live in a house on Jefferson Street.
- How much is your rent?
- Too much. $730.00 a month.
- That's a lot!

92 / *Here to Stay in the USA*

What's in the Picture?
Legal Advice
Talk about the picture with your classmates and teacher.

FREE LEGAL ADVICE
AYUDA LEGAL GRATIS
LANDLORD-TENANT

Student Space
Write your own words here.

Housing / 93

Communication Strategies

> If you can't understand a landlord or lawyer, ask for a **translator**.

I'm raising the rent next month.

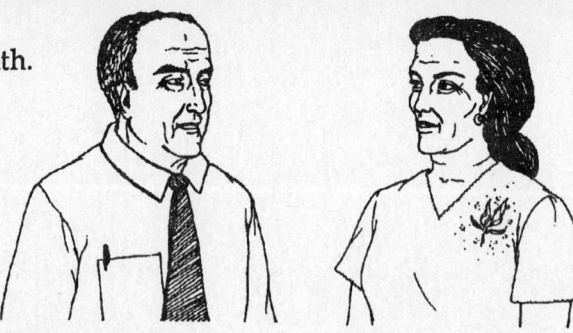

Excuse me, I need a translator.

Sign the lease right here.

My friend will translate for me.

What's the problem?

Excuse me, can you speak Spanish?

I don't speak Spanish. I don't have a translator.

Thank you. I'll come back tomorrow.

Communication Strategies

Your Gas and Electric Bill

Every month the gas and electric company sends you a bill. The bill tells you how much money you must pay. It tells you when the money is due.

Read the bill below. Answer the questions under the bill.

Davis Gas and Electric Company

Questions? Call our office at:
13 Central Street
Miami, FL 33153
(305) 555-9211

Your Account Number
5D00003

December 1990

TOMAS HERNANDEZ
2900 WALKER ST.
MIAMI, FL 33153

ELEC MTR NO.   E99999

Type of Service	SERVICE PERIOD From	To	Billing Days	METER READING Prior	Present	Reading Difference	Multiplier	GAS-TERMS* ELEC-KWH	Amount
ELEC	11/28	12/27	29	57056	57607	551	1	551	39.12

ENERGY COMMISSION TAX .11
TOTAL CURRENT CHARGES 39.23
PREVIOUS BALANCE 28.21
12/08 PAYMENT - THANK YOU 28.21
TOTAL AMOUNT NOW DUE $39.23

BASELINE QUANTITIES   ELECTRIC —   896.1 KWHRS
BASELINE USAGE   551.0 KWHRS @ $0.07099
OVER BASELINE USAGE   0.0 KWHRS @ 0.11720

AIR CONDITIONING YOUR HOME? SET THE THERMOSTAT AT 78 DEGREES TO SAVE ELECTRICITY. CLEAN OR REPLACE THE FILTERS REGULARLY.

BILL PERIOD	GAS THERMS Days	Billed	THERMS Per Day	ELECTRIC KWH Days	Billed	KWH Per Day
THIS MONTH THIS YEAR				29	551	19.0
THIS MONTH LAST YEAR				30	560	20.1

Information for comparing your daily use with last year's   THIS BILL IS NOW DUE AND PAYABLE

FORM 61-4461 REV 1-88

Monthly Bill

Answer the questions on the lines below.

1. Who is being billed? _Tomas Hernandez_

2. What is his account number? _____

3. How much is the bill? _____

4. What is the phone number of the Gas and Electric Company? _____

5. When is the bill due? _____

Housing / 95

Review Activity

Picture Story

Look at the pictures. Talk about the story in a group. Tell your story to the class.

96 / *Here to Stay in the USA*

UNIT NINE

Health

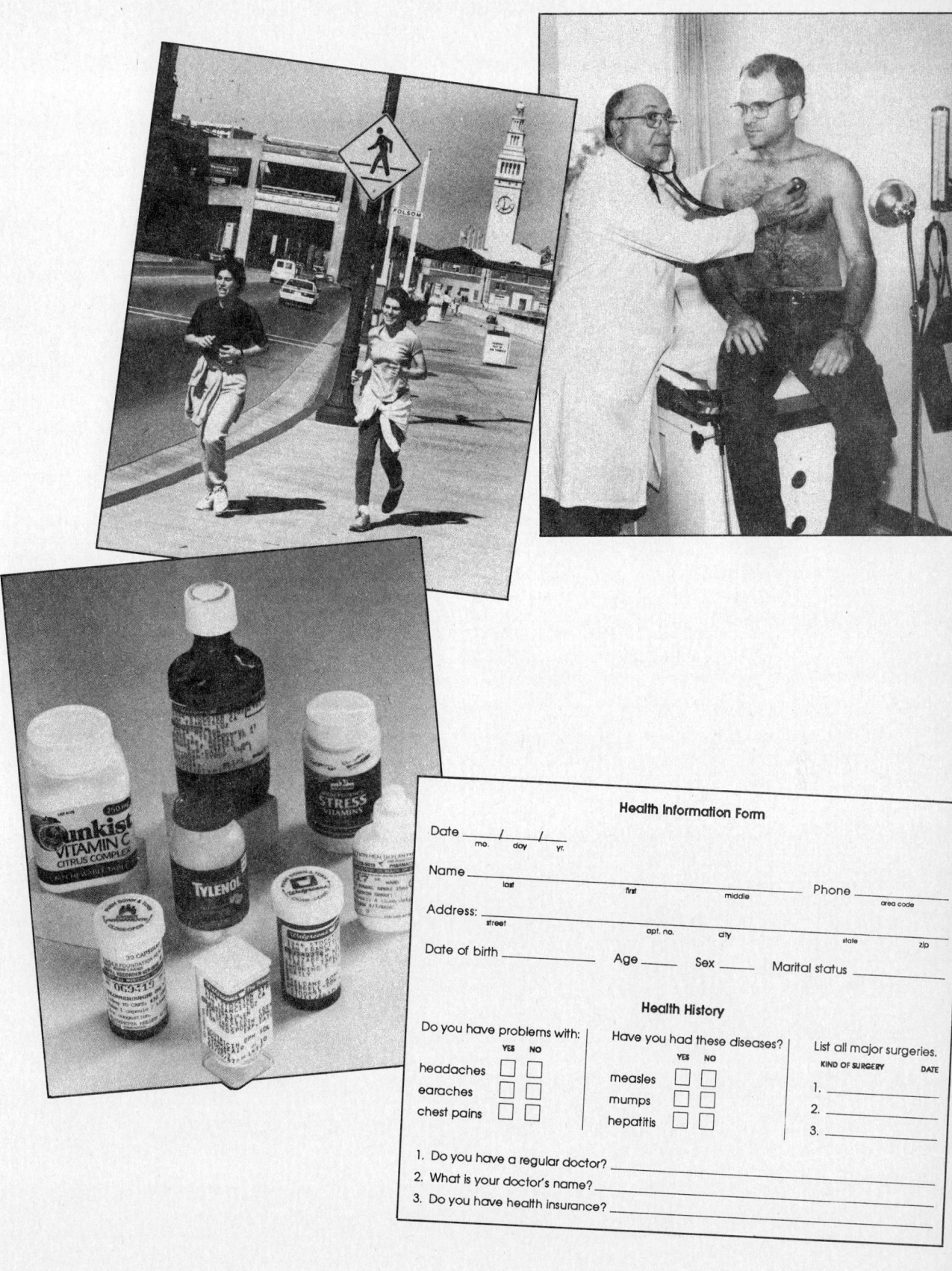

Reading 1
Feeling Sick

Key Words and Phrases

| sick | cough | drugstore | buy |
| medicine | label | twice a day | meals |

1. Suzanna Ibarra is sick.

2. She has a cough.

3. She goes to the drugstore.

4. She buys cough medicine.

5. She reads the label on the bottle.

6. It says, "Take two teaspoons every four hours."

Reading 2
An Appointment
Key Words and Phrases

need	medical examination	call
clinic	talk	nurse
price	make	appointment

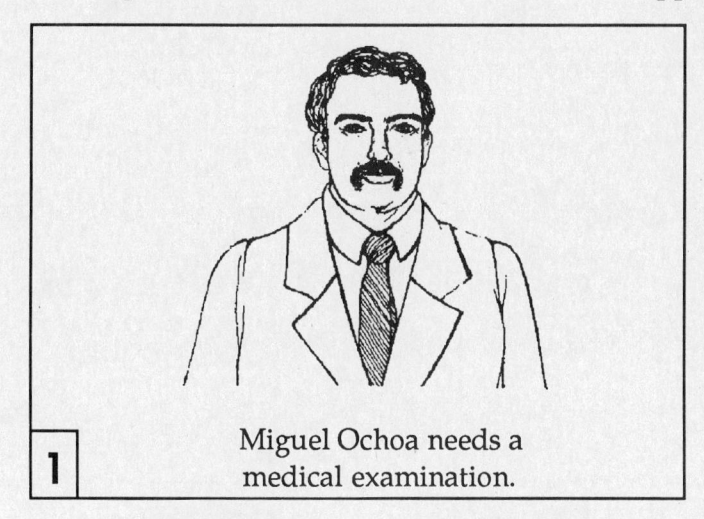

1. Miguel Ochoa needs a medical examination.
2. He calls the clinic.
3. He talks to the nurse. 
4. He asks about the price. 
5. He makes an appointment. 
6. Mr. MIGUEL OCHOA 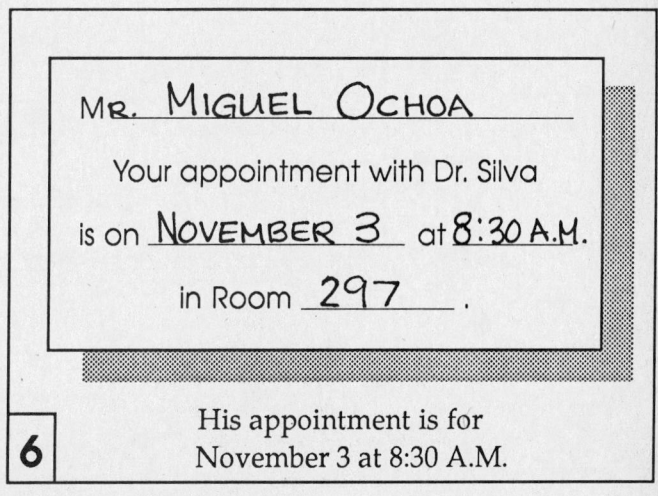
   Your appointment with Dr. Silva is on NOVEMBER 3 at 8:30 A.M. in Room 297.

   His appointment is for November 3 at 8:30 A.M.

Health / 99

Vocabulary Pictures
Body Parts

Look at the words and picture below. Label the body parts. Work with your classmates.

head	hair	eyes	nose	mouth	teeth
throat	neck	shoulders	chest	arms	hands
fingers	stomach	hips	legs	knees	feet

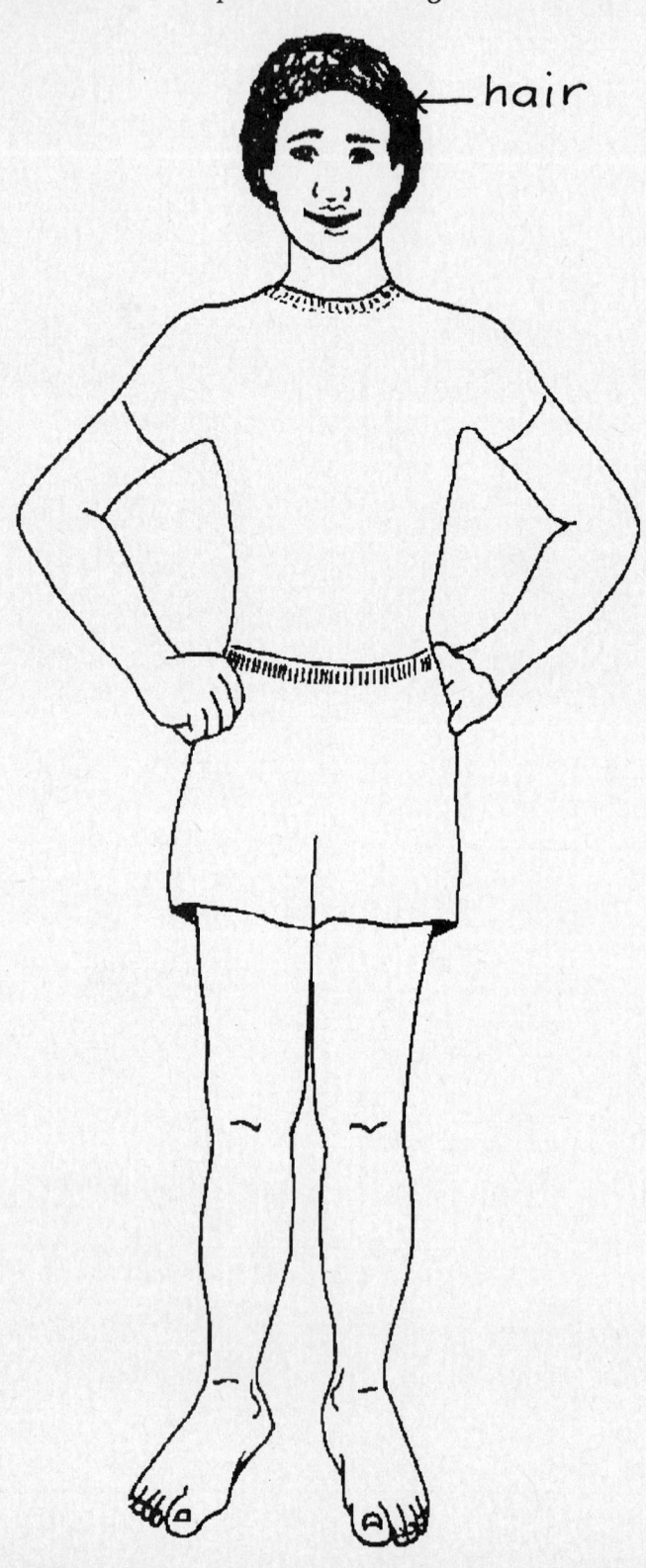

hair

Action Scripts
Classroom Calisthenics

Script 1

1. Take a deep breath.
2. Raise your right hand.
3. Raise your left hand.
4. Touch your toes.
5. Touch your knees.
6. Put your hands on your hips.

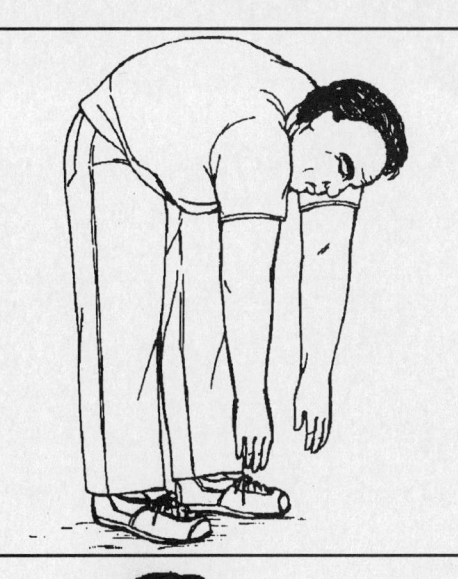

Script 2

1. Hold your arms out straight.
2. Make three small circles with your arms.
3. Make three big circles with your arms.
4. Put your arms down.
5. Relax.

Script 3

1. Put your hands on your hips.
2. Spread your feet apart.
3. Touch your left foot with your right hand.
4. Straighten up.
5. Touch your right foot with your left hand.
6. Straighten up.
7. Do it three times.
8. Relax.

Health / 101

Common Health Problems

Look at the pictures below. Answer the questions at the bottom of the page.

backache    headache    toothache

stomachache    earache    chest pains

What about You?

Put a check (✔) in the column that tells how you feel.

	Often	Sometimes	Never
1. Do you ever have earaches?	_____	_____	_____
2. Do you ever get headaches?	_____	_____	_____
3. Do you ever get stomachaches?	_____	_____	_____
4. Do you ever get toothaches?	_____	_____	_____
5. Do you smoke?	_____	_____	_____
6. Do you drink?	_____	_____	_____
7. Do you exercise?	_____	_____	_____
8. Do you go to the doctor for a checkup?	_____	_____	_____

> Ms. __GOMEZ__
>
> Your appointment with Dr. Silva
> is on __Thursday, April 12__ at __8 A.M.__
> in Room __304__.

Listen to This!

Your teacher will read the sentences below. Listen and circle the right answer in each box.

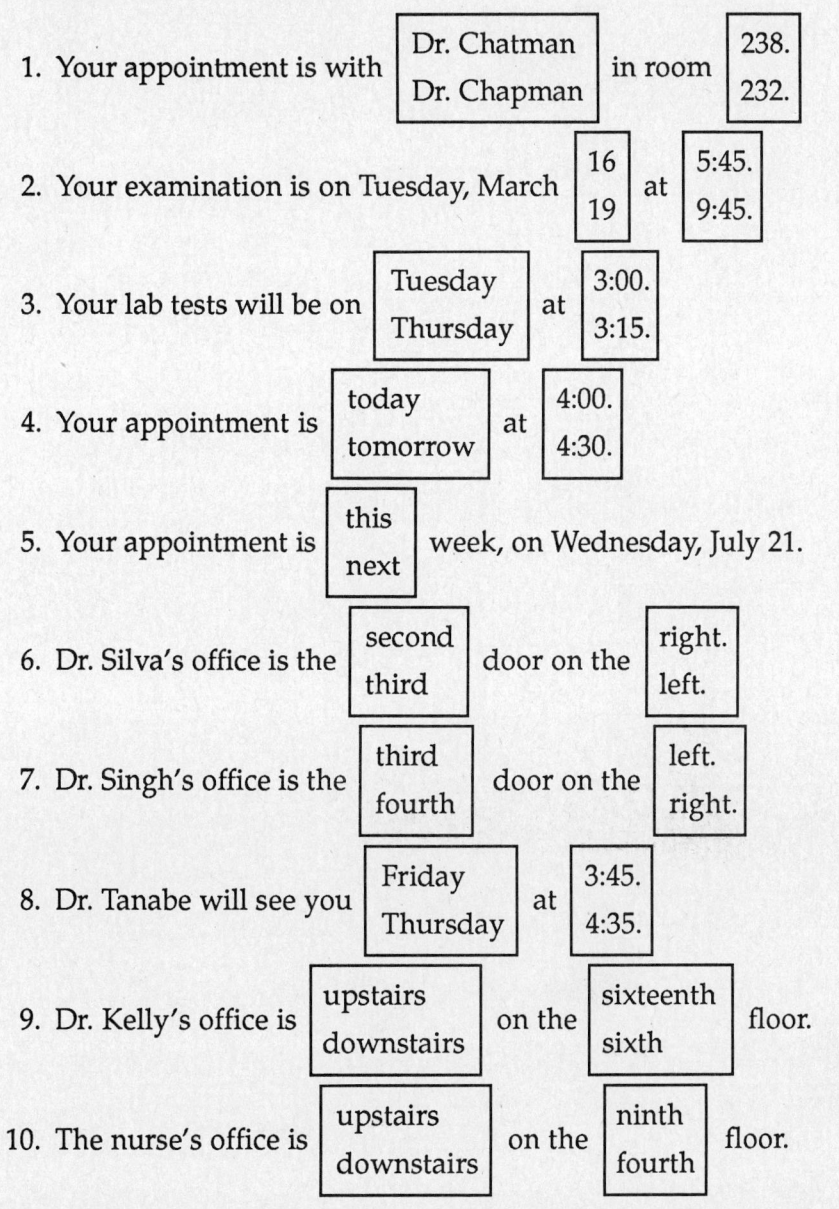

1. Your appointment is with [Dr. Chatman / Dr. Chapman] in room [238. / 232.]

2. Your examination is on Tuesday, March [16 / 19] at [5:45. / 9:45.]

3. Your lab tests will be on [Tuesday / Thursday] at [3:00. / 3:15.]

4. Your appointment is [today / tomorrow] at [4:00. / 4:30.]

5. Your appointment is [this / next] week, on Wednesday, July 21.

6. Dr. Silva's office is the [second / third] door on the [right. / left.]

7. Dr. Singh's office is the [third / fourth] door on the [left. / right.]

8. Dr. Tanabe will see you [Friday / Thursday] at [3:45. / 4:35.]

9. Dr. Kelly's office is [upstairs / downstairs] on the [sixteenth / sixth] floor.

10. The nurse's office is [upstairs / downstairs] on the [ninth / fourth] floor.

Health / 103

Health Talk

Read the dialogs below. Practice them with a classmate.

- How do you feel?
- I have a cold.

- And how do you feel today?
- Not so good. My back hurts.

- How do you feel?
- Fine. How about you?

104 / *Here to Stay in the USA*

What's in the Picture?

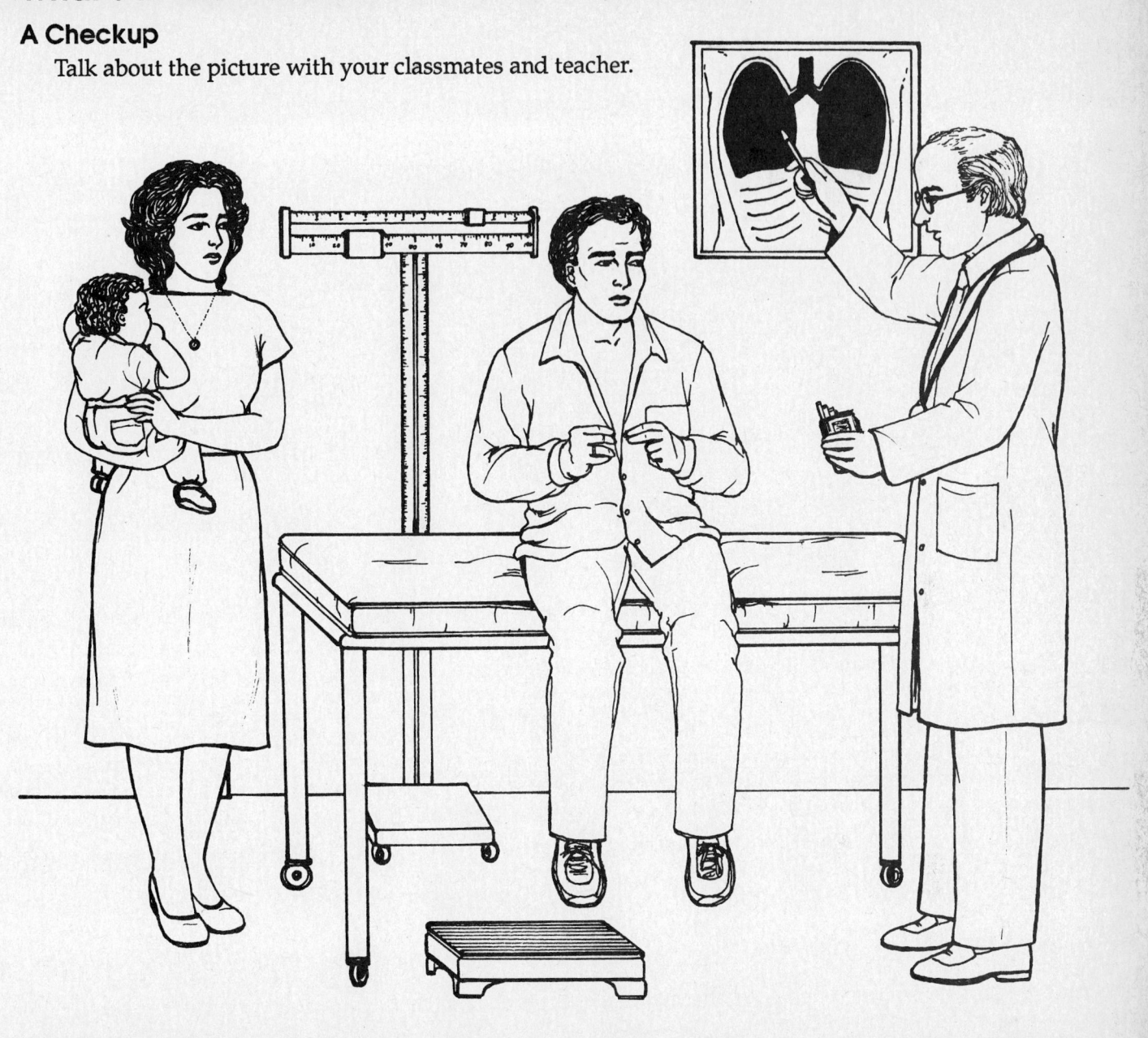

A Checkup
Talk about the picture with your classmates and teacher.

Student Space
Write your own words here.

Communication Strategies

> When you go to a clinic, say your **name** and the **time** of your appointment. State the **reason** you came.

May I help you?

My name is Oscar Gomez. I have an appointment at 3:45.

Do you have an appointment?

No, I want to make one for my son. He has the flu.

May I help you?

Yes. I want to make an appointment. My name is Minh Tam.

What's the matter?

I have a fever. My name is Marissa Espinosa. My appointment is at 3:00.

106 / *Here to Stay in the USA*

Working Out

Lots of Americans like to exercise for their health. They enjoy swimming, jogging and other exercises. Young and old people like to exercise. Look at the words and pictures below. Answer the questions at the bottom of the page.

bicycling    jogging    weightlifting

swimming    basketball    walking

Do You Like to Exercise?

Put a check (✔) in the column that tells about yourself.

	Often	Sometimes	Never
1. Do you exercise?	_____	_____	_____
2. Do you swim?	_____	_____	_____
3. Do you jog?	_____	_____	_____
4. Do you walk?	_____	_____	_____
5. Do you play basketball?	_____	_____	_____
6. What kind of exercise do you like?	_____	_____	_____

Health / 107

Conversation and Cooperation

Ask your friends what kind of exercise they like. Ask them how much they exercise. Write their answers below.

Name	Exercise	Days	Time

Review Activity

Fill out the health form with information about yourself.

Health Information Form

Date ____/____/____
      mo. day yr.

Name _____ Phone _____
       last   first   middle

Address: _____
          street   apt. no.   city   state   zip

Date of birth _____ Age _____ Sex _____ Marital status _____

Health History

Do you have problems with:

	YES	NO
headaches	☐	☐
earaches	☐	☐
chest pains	☐	☐

Have you had these diseases?

	YES	NO
measles	☐	☐
mumps	☐	☐
hepatitis	☐	☐

List all major surgeries.

KIND OF SURGERY   DATE

1. _____
2. _____
3. _____

1. Do you have a regular doctor? _____
2. What is your doctor's name? _____
3. Do you have health insurance? _____

Here to Stay in the USA

UNIT TEN

Transportation

Reading 1

Taking the Bus

Key Words and Phrases

take the bus	wait	bus stop
get on	pay	get off

1. Teresa takes the bus to work.
2. She waits at the bus stop.
3. She gets on the bus.
4. She pays 75 cents.
5. She gets off the bus.
6. It takes 40 minutes to get to work.

110 / *Here to Stay in the USA*

Reading 2
The Freeway

Key Words and Phrases

| take | freeway | route | get on |
| get off | exit | leave | parking lot |

1. Oscar takes the freeway to work.
2. He takes Route 5. 
3. He gets on at 19th Street. 
4. He gets off at the Fargo Avenue exit. 
5. He leaves his car in a parking lot. 
6. It takes him 55 minutes to get to work. 

Transportation / 111

Vocabulary Pictures
Street Signs

Write the correct letter under each sign.

a. Stop
b. Yield
c. Pedestrians crossing
d. One way
e. No left turn
f. Railroad crossing
g. Bicycle route
h. 55 miles an hour
i. Children crossing
j. Men working
k. Do not enter
l. Handicapped Parking

1. C
2. _____ 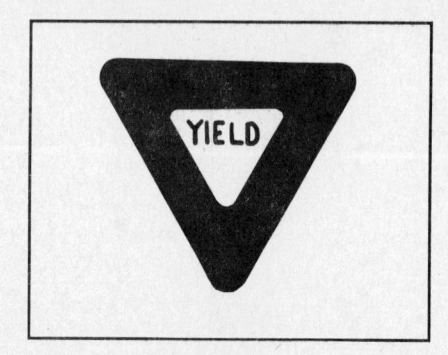
3. _____ 
4. _____ 
5. _____ 
6. _____ 
7. _____ 
8. _____ 
9. _____ 
10. _____ 
11. _____ 
12. _____ 

112 / *Here to Stay in the USA*

Action Scripts

Gas Station

Script 1 *Buying Gasoline*
(Materials: use a desk as a car. Use another desk as the gas pump.)

1. Get out of the car.
2. Walk to the counter.
3. Pay $5.00 for gas.
4. Walk back to the car.
5. Take off your gas cap.
6. Pick up the gas pump.
7. Put the gas pump in the gas tank.
8. Pump $5.00 of gas.
9. Put the gas pump back.
10. Get in the car and drive away.

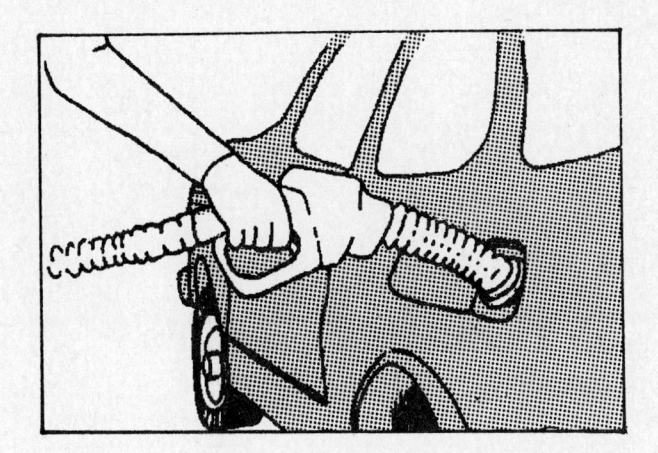

Script 2 *Car Problems*
(Materials: desk as a car, *Yellow Pages*)

1. Your car won't start.
2. Get out of the car.
3. Lift up the hood.
4. Look at the engine.
5. Get in the car.
6. Try and start it again.
7. It won't start. Get out of the car.
8. Pick up a *Yellow Pages*.
9. Look up "Service Stations."
10. Call a service station.

Bus Schedule

Read the bus schedule below. Answer the questions under the schedule.

Bus 95A — Monday Through Friday   A.M.

Richmond Mall	181st St.	199th St.	Thomas St.	225th St.
6:30	6:45	7:00	7:15	7:30
6:45	7:00	7:15	7:30	7:45
7:00	7:15	7:30	7:45	8:00
8:15	8:30	8:45	9:00	9:15

Bus 95A — Saturday and Sunday   A.M.

Richmond Mall	181st St.	199th St.	Thomas St.	225th St.
8:15		8:45	9:00	9:15
9:15		9:45	10:00	10:15

Reading a Bus Schedule

Write the answers on the lines below.

1. What time is the first bus on Monday? __6:30__
2. What time is the first bus on Saturday? _____
3. Does the 95A stop at 225th Street? _____
4. Does the 95A stop at 181st on Saturday? _____
5. What time is the last bus on Sunday? _____

What about You?

Write about yourself on the lines below.

1. Do you ever take the bus? _____
2. Do you own a car? _____
3. How do you get to work? _____
4. How long does it take? _____
5. How much does it cost? _____

Here to Stay in the USA

Listen to This!

Your teacher will read the sentences below. Listen and circle the right answer in each box.

How do I get to the hospital?

1. Go straight for [three / 13] blocks.

2. At the light, make a [right. / left.]

3. Make a [left turn / U-turn] at Beasley Street.

Which bus goes to Fullerton Road?

1. Take the [#27. / #37.]

2. Stay on for [four / five] stops.

3. Get off at Carver Street and transfer to the number [12 / 21] bus.

Conversation and Cooperation

Choose two locations and fill in the information on **time** and **costs**. Call the bus station, train station, or airport for information.

Example:

From: <u>Los Angeles</u>

To: <u>San Francisco</u> By: <u>bus</u> Costs: <u>$44.95</u> Time: <u>7 hours 55 minutes</u>

1. From _____

   To: _____ By: _____ Costs: _____ Time: _____

2. From _____

   To: _____ By: _____ Costs: _____ Time: _____

3. From _____

   To: _____ By: _____ Costs: _____ Time: _____

Transportation / 115

Transportation Talk
Read the dialogs below. Practice them with a classmate.

- Excuse me, where does this bus go?
- To 44th Street and Jackson Avenue.

- What's the fare?
- 75 cents.

- Do you drive?
- No, I don't.

- How did you get to Miami?
- By plane. I flew from San Francisco.

116 / *Here to Stay in the USA*

What's in the Picture?

Getting a Ticket
Talk about the picture with your classmates and teacher.

Student Space
Write your own words here.

Transportation / 117

Communication Strategies

> If you're not sure what you hear,
> **repeat** the words you're not sure of.

Go to 4th Avenue.   To 1st Avenue?

Go three blocks and make a right.   Three blocks and a right?

Take 560 South for three exits.   560 South? Four exits?

Take the number 90 bus.   Number 19?

118 / *Here to Stay in the USA*

The Freeway

Americans like to drive. Do you know how to drive? Do you have a driver's license? Read the map below. Answer the questions under the map.

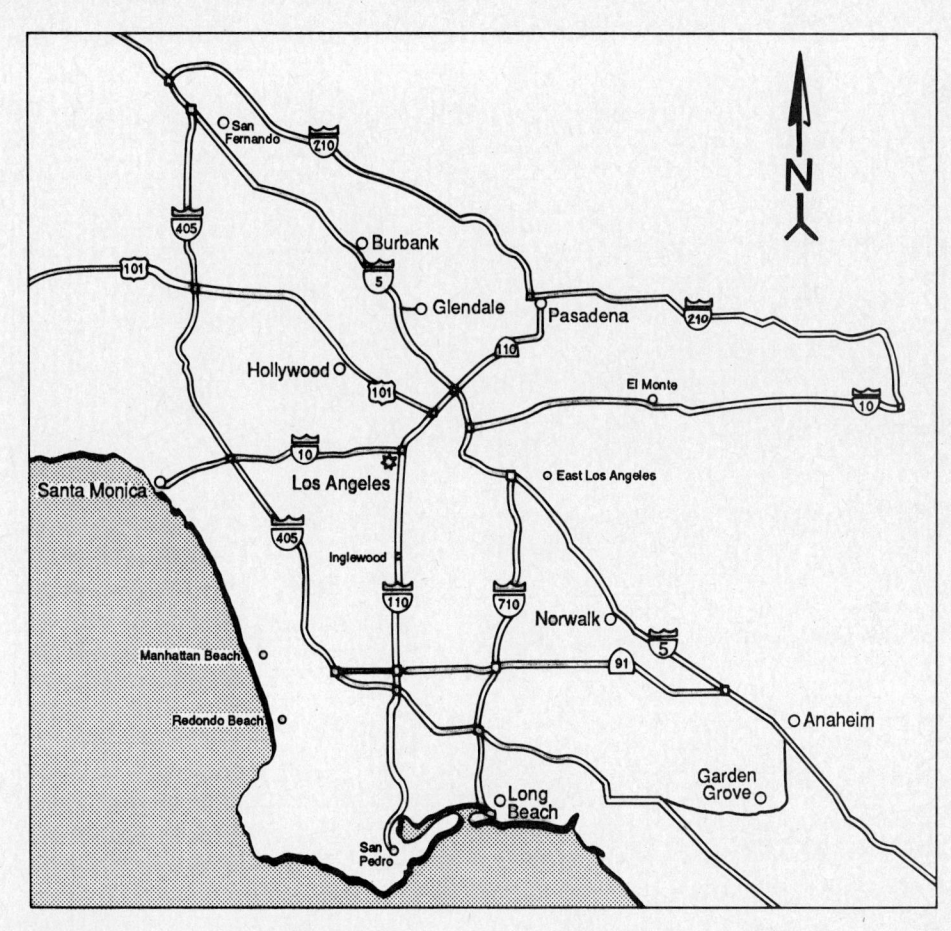

How Do You Get There?

Write the answers on the lines below.

1. How do you get from Los Angeles to Burbank?

   Highway 110 to Highway 5

2. How do you get from Los Angeles to Santa Monica?

   _____

3. How do you get from Anaheim to Santa Monica?

   _____

4. How do you get from Long Beach to El Monte?

   _____

5. How do you get from Inglewood to Hollywood?

   _____

Transportation / 119

Review Activity

Picture Story

Look at the pictures. Talk about the story in a group. Tell your story to the class.

120 / *Here to Stay in the USA*

UNIT ELEVEN

All about America

Reading 1

The U.S. Constitution

Key Words and Phrases

U.S. Constitution	written	guarantee	freedom
speech	religion	press	highest law

1 The U.S. Constitution was written in 1787.

2 It guarantees American freedoms.

3 Americans have freedom of speech.

4 Americans have freedom of religion.

5 Americans have freedom of the press.

6 The Constitution is the highest law in the land.

122 / *Here to Stay in the USA*

Reading 2
Rights and Responsibilities

Key Words and Phrases

| citizens | rights | responsibility | live |
| work | passport | vote | teach |

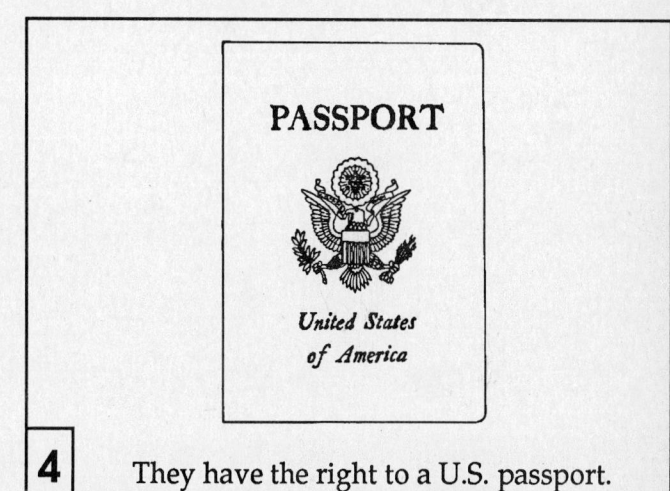

1. American citizens have **rights** and **responsibilities**.
2. They have the right to live in the United States. 
3. They have the right to work. 
4. They have the right to a U.S. passport.
5. They have a responsibility to vote. 
6. They have a responsibility to teach their children about the United States. 

All about America / 123

Vocabulary Pictures
American Landmarks

Write the correct letter under each picture.
- a. The White House
- b. The Statue of Liberty
- c. The Empire State Building
- d. The Liberty Bell
- e. The United States Capitol
- f. Mount Rushmore

1. _a_

2. _____

3. _____

4. _____

5. _____

6. _____

124 / *Here to Stay in the USA*

Four American Presidents

Read about each President. Answer the questions at the bottom of the page.

George Washington
- He was the first President.
- He is called "the father of our country."

Thomas Jefferson
- He was the third President.
- He wrote the Declaration of Independence.

Abraham Lincoln
- He was the 16th President.
- He ended slavery in the United States.

George Bush
- He is the President today.
- He is the 41st U.S. President.

Questions about the Presidents

Write the answers on the lines below.

1. Who was the first President? _____

2. Who wrote the Declaration of Independence? _____

3. Who ended slavery in the United States? _____

4. Who is the President today? _____

5. Who is the leader of your native country? _____

All about America / 125

Talking about America

Read the dialogs below. Practice them with a classmate.

- America is work, work, work.
- America is fun for me.
- America is rich.
- America is rich and poor.
- America is education.
- America is crime.
- America is TV and fast food.
- America is freedom.

126 / *Here to Stay in the USA*

What's in the Picture?

The Right to Vote

Talk about the picture with your classmates and teacher.

YOUR VOTE IS YOUR VOICE
SU VOTO ES SU VOZ

Student Space

Write your own words here.

All about America / 127

Communication Strategies

> Bring **identification cards** with you when you go to a **government office** or when you **apply for a job**.

May I see your identification, please?   Here's my driver's license.

Do you have any I.D.?   Yes, here's my work I.D.

Do you have legal identification?   Yes, I have a green card.

May I see your identification, please?   Here. I have a passport.

128 / *Here to Stay in the USA*

Four Famous Americans of the 20th Century

Read about each famous American. Answer the questions at the bottom of the page.

Martin Luther King, Jr.
- 1929–1968
- Black American
- Civil rights leader

John F. Kennedy
- 1917–1963
- 35th President
- Assassinated in 1963

Helen Keller
- 1880–1968
- American writer
- Advocate for the handicapped

Cesar Chavez
- 1927–
- Mexican American
- Farm worker leader

Famous People from Your Native Country

Write the answers on the lines below.

1. Who is a famous man from your native country? _____

2. Who is a famous woman from your native country? _____

All about America

Famous Places

Find these famous places on the map.
Write the correct letter under each picture.

- a. The Golden Gate Bridge
- b. The Empire State Building
- c. The White House
- d. Grand Canyon
- e. Hollywood
- f. The Liberty Bell

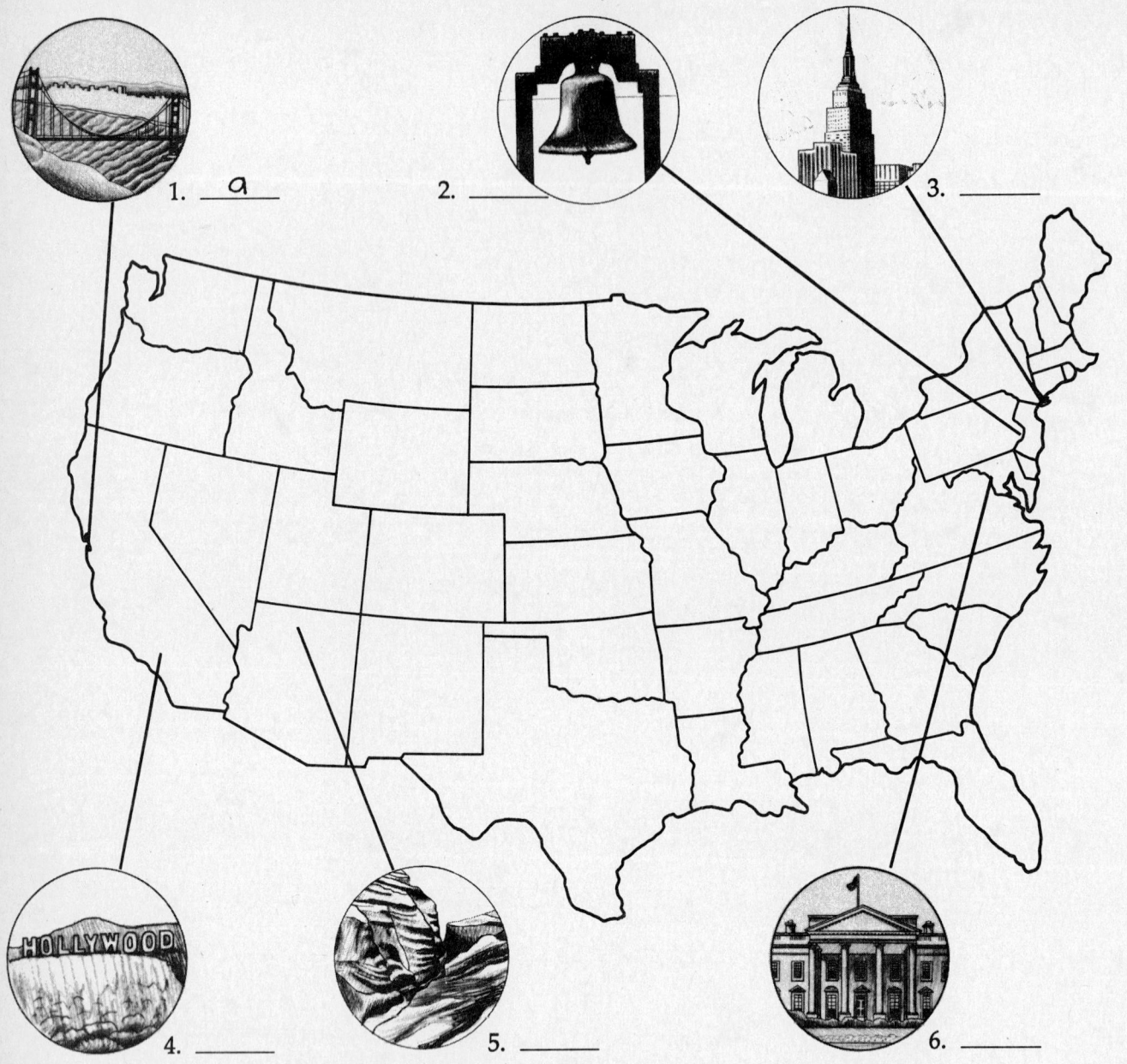

1. _a_   2. _____   3. _____

4. _____   5. _____   6. _____

Famous Places in Your Native Country

Write three famous places in your native country on the lines below.

1. _____
2. _____
3. _____

130 / *Here to Stay in the USA*

The United States Flag

The U.S. flag is red, white, and blue. It has 50 stars. It has 13 stripes. Read the Pledge of Allegiance and the *Star-Spangled Banner* with your classmates and teacher.

The Pledge of Allegiance

I pledge allegiance to the flag of the United States of America and to the Republic for which it stands, one nation, under God, indivisible, with liberty and justice for all.

The Star-Spangled Banner

Oh, say, can you see, by the dawn's early light,
What so proudly we hailed at the twilight's last gleaming;
Whose broad stripes and bright stars, through the perilous fight
O'er the ramparts we watched, were so gallantly streaming;
And the rocket's red glare, the bombs bursting in air,
Gave proof through the night that our flag was still there.
Oh, say, does that star-spangled banner yet wave
O'er the land of the free and the home of the brave?

All about America

Conversation and Cooperation

Write down some things in America that are different from your native country. Write down some things that are the same.

Different	Same
_____	_____
_____	_____
_____	_____
_____	_____
_____	_____
_____	_____

Review Activity

Write the answers on the lines below.

1. Who was the first President of the United States? _____

2. Who is the President of the United States today? _____

3. What is the highest law of the land? _____

4. What are the colors of the U.S. flag? _____

5. How many stars are in the U.S. flag? _____

Review Questions

Units One Through Eleven

1. What is your full name? _____
2. What is your father's name? _____
3. What is your mother's name? _____
4. What is your social security number? _____
5. How many people are in your family? _____
6. How many states are in the United States? _____
7. What is the capital of the United States? _____
8. What is the capital of your state? _____
9. What languages do you speak? _____
10. When is America's birthday? _____
11. When is Martin Luther King Day? _____
12. How do you report an accident? _____
13. Where can you buy a money order? _____
14. Do you live in an apartment? _____
15. What is your landlord's name? _____
16. Do you own a car? _____
17. Do you have a driver's license? _____
18. Who was the first President of the United States? _____
19. Who is the President today? _____
20. What are the colors of the U.S. flag? _____
21. How many stars in the U.S. flag? _____
22. How many stripes in the U.S. flag? _____
23. What are the colors of your native country's flag? _____
24. What is one right that American citizens have? _____
25. What is the highest law in the land? _____